IBN FADLAN'S JOURNEY TO RUSSIA

A Tenth-Century Traveler
from Baghdad
to the Volga River

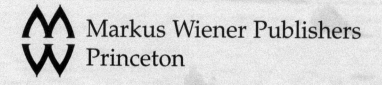

M
W Markus Wiener Publishers
Princeton

Ibn Fadlan's Journey to Russia

translated with commentary by

RICHARD N. FRYE

To Eden, my catalyst

Copyright © 2005 by Richard N. Frye
Third printing, 2010

For information, write to: Markus Wiener Publishers
231 Nassau Street, Princeton, NJ 08542
www.markuswiener.com

Cover illustration by Maria Madonna Davidoff, adapted from a painting of a qadi in his tent in the *Maqamat* of al-Hariri.

Library of Congress Cataloging-in-Publication Data

Ibn Faḍlān, Aḥmad, fl. 922.
  [Kitāb ilá malik al-Ṣaqālibah. English]
  Ibn Fadlan's journey to Russia : a tenth-century traveler from Baghdad to the Volga River / translated with commentary by Richard N. Frye.
    Includes bibliographical references.
    ISBN-13: 978-1-55876-366-1 (pbk. : alk. paper)
    ISBN-10: 1-55876-366-X (pbk. : alk. paper)
    ISBN-13: 978-1-55876-365-4 (hardcover : alk. paper)
    ISBN-10: 1-55876-365-1 (hardcover : alk. paper)
    1. Tatarstan (Russia)—Description and travel. 2. Asia, Central—Description and travel. 3. Bulgars (Turkic people)—Russia (Federation)—Volga River Region—History. 4. Ibn Faḍlān, Aḥmad, fl. 922—Travel—Asia, Central. 5. Volga River Region (Russia)—History.
    I. Frye, Richard Nelson, 1920– . II. Title.
  DK511.T17I2313 2005
  914.7'45042—dc22

                                                        2005013216

Markus Wiener Publishers books are printed in the United States of America on acid-free paper, and meet the guidelines for permanence and durability of the Committee on Production Guidelines for Book Longevity of the Council on Library Resources.

Contents

Preface

In 1946, upon returning to Harvard University after three years in the Middle East, my advisor, Robert P. Blake, Professor of Byzantine History, asked me to collaborate with him in writing an article on Ibn Fadlan's travels from the Caliph in Baghdad to the king of the Bulghars on the Volga River (Blake and Frye 1949). An Arabic manuscript had been found in the city of Meshhed, reportedly the original version of a text that had been published twice already, with translations in German and Russian. At the same time, Professor Carleton Coon, of the Department of Anthropology, requested me to translate the account of Ibn Fadlan concerning the Rus as found in the *Geographical Dictionary of Yaqut* (Wüstenfeld 1866) for his reader in general anthropology (Coon 1948).

Fifty-eight years later, Markus Wiener proposed that I present these translations, plus notes and additions, in the form of a popular book, without the critical apparatus of variant readings and diacritical marks on Arabic words, to allow the educated lay reader or student to benefit from the writing of the earliest Arab traveler to record information about the Russian heartland. I agreed, with the added suggestion that a major thrust of the writing should be on trade between the Near East and both Russia and China, from ancient as well as early Islamic times. Inasmuch as there is an enormous body of literature on Ibn Fadlan's account of the Rus, I have refrained from going into detail on this subject. Instead I have attached several appendices to the translation, plus notes dealing mainly with trade and commerce as well as politics.

I especially wish to thank Dr. James E. McKeithen for his gracious permission to allow me to use the translations of the sec-

tions on the Bashkirs and the Bulghars from his Ph.D. thesis at
Indiana University in 1979. I have found his translation accurate
and thus saw no need to retranslate these sections myself,
although I have consulted the text and other translations for disputed passages. Also, in the last part of my translation of the
section on the Khazars, Professor Wolfhart Heinrichs of Harvard
helped me with some questions on readings and translations of
the Arabic text, for which I am grateful. As noted above, the
translation I made in 1946 (Blake and Frye 1946) has been used
here, since the original article is difficult to find. The full translation here makes no pretensions of great originality; it is
frankly a *travail de vulgarisation,* and the specialist who is interested in variant readings of the Arabic, or extensive notes on
various parts of the work, should refer to the editions of Zeki-
Velidi Togan (1939) and A. P. Kovalevskii (1939), or to other
items noted in the bibliography.

Additions to the text, usually to elucidate the translation,
have been given in brackets. Otherwise, the commentary at the
end of the translation is intended to explain some passages of
the text without aiming to serve as anything like a complete exe-
gesis. Long marks over vowels, dots under letters, and other
marks of Arabic words have been omitted, inasmuch as one
who does not know Arabic will find them unnecessary, while
scholars will realize what is intended.

Much has been written about portions of the account of Ibn
Fadlan, especially about the Rus, and summaries of the work of
Ibn Fadlan exist, but I believe this is the first complete English
translation to be published of what we have of his account. I
hope that a wide audience will appreciate this early and original
travel account.

Introduction

In the tenth century, two new religious faiths emerged in present-day Russia. The inhabitants of Kiev accepted Greek Orthodox Christianity from Byzantine missionaries, while to the east, on the Volga River, the kingdom of the Bulghars turned to Islam. Both faiths have continued to the present in these locations: today the Tatars of Tataristan in Russia, and their capital of Kazan, are the successors of the Bulghars. Although few written accounts exist of the conversion of the inhabitants of the Kievan state to Christianity, even less is known about the Bulghars. Fortunately, one source about early Islam in that kingdom has survived: a report by Ahmad ibn Fadlan ibn al-'Abbas ibn Rashid ibn Hammad, an envoy from the 'Abbasid Caliph in Baghdad to the king of the Bulghars on the upper Volga River. Since his trip occurred during a specific period of time, it is a historical as well as an ethnological document.

Written in Arabic in the tenth century, Ibn Fadlan's account of his voyage to the north is a record of his observations, uncharacteristically devoid of the flattery and exaggeration one might find in a document presented to the Caliphal court. His unparalleled eyewitness account gives us valuable information about the customs and beliefs of the tribes he met on his voyage to the realm of the Bulghars. It is also the earliest notice of the customs of the Rus whom he encountered. Scholars have long debated whether this latter term refers to Swedish Vikings, called Varangians, or to a band of traders who were a mixture of Slavs and Vikings. The name "Varangian" apparently derives from an old Scandinavian word denoting those who shared an oath to cooperate and share profits in their trade. It was a synonym for the earlier Rus, as seen in Byzantine sources of the eleventh century.

Trade between the Baltic and northern Russia, and between the Near East and India, was an early and significant route for the exchange of ideas and fashions, as well as goods. The information provided by Ibn Fadlan is a welcome addition to the results obtained from archaeology, as for example the excavation of Itil, capital of the Khazars on the lower Volga near present Astrakhan. The volume of trade along the northwest-southeast route may be compared with the trade to China along the so-called Silk Road. Yet while ample information exists about the merchants who dominated the routes between the west and China (a 2002 book by Étienne de la Vaissière is one very good account), as far as I know there is no comparable, up-to-date book on the trade between the Volga and the Near East.

While Ibn Fadlan's report is the most complete account to survive, it is significant to note that Muslim merchants had also traveled to the north and had made observations on their travels, which were reported in geographies such as those by Istakhri, Ibn Hauqal, Muqaddasi and Mas'udi. Such information, however, is meager, and the scanty details it provides—such as mention of the northern lights and the short days during winter—cannot compare with those found in Ibn Fadlan's book.

A note on the names

In the past, family names did not exist in Arabic. Rather, one was identified as the son (*ibn*) or daughter (*bint*) of a father, or as the father (*abu*) or mother (*uma*) of a child. Sometimes, to further identify a person, an appellation would be added, such as "al-Fadl" (the superior one), which then became part of that person's name. The definite article in Arabic is *al-*.

Glossary of
Terms and Titles

amir: Arabic title commander or governor

beg or beh: originally high Iranian title, but used for the aristocracy by Turks; today simply the equivalent of "mister"

da'i: Arabic word referring to the chief of missionaries of heretical Islamic sects

dang or *danik*: copper coin, one sixth of a *dirham*

dinar: Islamic gold coin (word from *denarius),* although sometimes used generally for *dirham*

farsakh: Persian measure equal to about six kilometers, but varying in different times and places

iqama: beginning of the prayer inside a mosque

jinn: Islamic supernatural beings who practice magic

jaushigir: Turkic title taken from *chavush,* "military commander"

khaqan: general Turko-Mongolian title of supreme chief of a tribal coalition

khutba: Arabic word for the invocation to the ruler at the beginning of prayer

kudarkin: Turkic title of the vice-regent of the *yabghu* or tribal chief

kundur: Uralic or Hungarian title of the assistant to the *khaqan*

mead: drink made of fermented honey (here the Arabic term *nabid* means any intoxicating drink)

mithqal: Islamic weight, usually over a dram or two grams

pustin: sheepskin coat usually worn by pastoralists up to the present in Central Asia

ratl or rital: heavy weight, varying from two to twenty pounds across places and times, but of unknown value in Khwarazm at this time

sultan: the caliph or his government; later, a secular ruler

tamga: sign similar to a signature, either personal or, more usually, signifying tribal affiliation or government certification

tarkhan: ancient title of nobility, possibly pre-Turkic but adopted by Turks

tekin: princely Turkic title; also a personal name

yabghu: old Turkic title of the chief of a tribe

yiltawar or *elteber*: Turkic title of the vassal ruler of the *khaqan*

yanal: Turkic title of a young prince or deputy of the tribal chief

yughrush: Turkic title, similar to vizier

CHAPTER I

Silver plate from the 8th–10th cent.

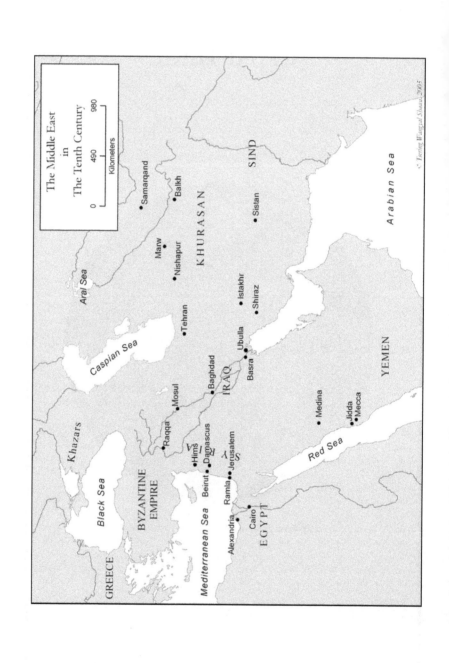

The Middle East
in
The Tenth Century

0   490   980
Kilometers

Aral Sea

Samarqand
Balkh

KHURASAN

Marw
Nishapur

SIND

Sistan

Caspian Sea

Istakhr
Shiraz

Tehran

Ubulla

Baghdad
Basra
IRAQ

Mosul

Raqqa

Khazars

Hims
Damascus
Jerusalem
S Y R I A

Arabian Sea

Medina

Jidda
Mecca

YEMEN

Red Sea

Black Sea

BYZANTINE
EMPIRE

Beirut
Ramla
Alexandria
Cairo
EGYPT

Mediterranean Sea

GREECE

Tsering Wangyal Shawa 2005

The Time and the Man

The early tenth century, when Ibn Fadlan lived, was the culmination of great changes in the Islamic world. Over a century had passed since the establishment of the 'Abbasid Caliphate in 750, and the Islamic religion was now firmly established from Spain to the frontiers of India, and to some extent in the southern part of the nomadic world of Inner Asia. The previous Umayyad Caliphate, with its capital in Damascus, had lasted only a century and has been characterized as an Arab kingdom, based on the customs and mores of the Arabian tribes at the time of the prophet Muhammad. By contrast, the successor caliphate —the 'Abbasids—has often been described as an Iranian dynasty because of the great influence of Iranians on the culture and institutions of the time.

This was much more than just a political change. Islamic civilization had been transformed from a society bound to Bedouin tribal mores into a manifold international culture. The Arab tribes that had dominated the scene abruptly disappear from the sources at this point in history, indicating a profound change of direction not just in politics but also in a religion that had been brought from the deserts of Arabia. As long ago as the fourteenth century, the Tunisian writer Ibn Khaldun, in his introduction to history, mentioned with astonishment the overwhelming number of Iranians who had laid the foundations of Islamic learning, science, and all the arts. Ibn Khaldun, it should be noted, neglected the important contributions of Syriac speakers of the "Fertile Crescent," who also made valuable additions to Islamic culture. As a matter of fact, it was not the Persians of western Iran, but more the inhabitants of eastern Iran and Central Asia, who were the first and main actors in this enterprise.

The reason for the greater influence of eastern Iran is not difficult to find. In western Iran, for a long time after 750, the population was still mainly Zoroastrian in religion, with Christian pockets here and there, while the Muslims (mainly Arab tribesmen and their clients) were concentrated in a few cities and towns, such as Qum and Ray. The different religious communities maintained almost a separate existence from each other, since to become a Muslim had meant to become an Arab, learn the Arabic language, and break with past traditions—as well as with one's family, if they did not also convert. Under the Sasanian Empire, the governing system known later in the Ottoman Empire as the *millet* system had come into being. Under this system, religious minorities were separated from the dominant Zoroastrians and given special jurisdictions. This meant that the Jews in the empire, as a minority religious community, were under the jurisdiction of the head of the community called the *resh galutha* (leader of the diaspora). Likewise, the Christians were under the authority of a patriarch. The Sasanian government dealt with the heads of these religious groups in cases of conflict between minorities and Zoroastrians, or conflicts with the state, and also when collecting taxes. On the other hand, the religious leader or his assistants handled internal problems within the group. Under the 'Abbasids, this system metamorphosed into an Islamic concept of Dhimmis—"people of the Book"—and infidels, or those without the Hebrew-Christian traditions. A form of this system has existed since 1980 in theocratic Iran, with religious minorities assigned one or two representatives in the parliament by the government.

In the east, however—in Khurasan and Central Asia—on the eve of the Islamic conquest, there had been no central government as in the Sasanian state. The various oases functioned like ancient Greek city-states, sometimes united but usually separate and hostile. There was no official or state religion, and Judaism, Christianity, Buddhism, Manichaeism, and various forms of paganism existed. Unlike in the west, merchants were both numerous and highly respected, and tolerance was a hallmark of the mercantile communities. This spirit of indulgence toward those of different beliefs created a milieu where exercise of the intellect and new ideas flourished. The ground was laid for the birth of a new Islamic culture when the oases were united under one rule of the Caliphate. Trade and commerce, which had flourished in the ninth century, experienced even greater impetus with the benevolent rule of the Samanids throughout the tenth century.

The far-flung 'Abbasid Caliphate suffered a breaking away of provinces in the ninth century. Egypt and North Africa came under the rule of the Fatimids, followers of a heretical movement called the Ismailis, whose descendants today are led by the Aga Khan. The Zaidis, who exist today in Yemen, have been characterized as a moderate branch of the Ismailis, meaning that they were more relaxed in their interpretations and practices of Islam. In the east, several provinces became independent in practice, although in theory, as we see in the account of Ibn Fadlan, they maintained allegiance to the Caliph in Baghdad. Khurasan and Central Asia came under the rule of the Samanid family and the dynasty that it established, with its capital in Bukhara. Under Ismail ibn Ahmad (892–907) the domain of the Samanids expanded over the Iranian plateau, and Bukhara became an intellectual center second only to Baghdad.

It was in the east that New Persian literature, written in the Arabic alphabet, was born. This spoken tongue already had replaced local languages and dialects. (Although attempts were made to write the Khwarazmian and Sogdian languages, as well as the dialect of Mazanderan, south of the Caspian Sea, in Arabic script, only Persian spread throughout Iran and Central Asia.) The monopoly that Arabic had as the only language of

IMPERIAL ROME
(black: Rome in the IX-X centuries)

CONSTANTINOPLE
in the IX-X centuries

PARIS at the end of the XIX century
(black: Paris in the IX-X centuries)

BAGHDAD in the IX-X centuries

Comparative sizes of some capital cities: Rome, Constantinople, Paris, and Baghdad

Muslims was broken, and a new ecumenical Islamic civilization came into being. This gave a new impetus to the spread of Islam on the steppes of inner Asia and into India. Arabic had acquired the status of a holy language, and its influence spread with the religion. Thus, it was in the east—where an Islamic Persian language was added to the plethora of literary, scientific, and legalistic writings of savants in Arabic—that Islam was transformed from a religion and culture bound to Arab mores into an international civilization. It is safe to say that Islamic learning came to fruition in this Central Asian region, for the number of scholars and writers from this area exceeded by far all others in the Islamic world stretching from the Atlantic to India.

The site of Baghdad was inhabited before Islam [but] pre-Islamic Baghdad had merely a localized function, in common with many . . . old inhabited centres. Al-Mansur was its real creator, and he called it 'Madinat as-Salam', the 'city of Peace'. Building was started in 762. Workmen were brought in from every quarter— more than 100,000 were employed at once—as well as specialists. These men were the city's earliest inhabitants, as well as its builders. And so in four years there arose a circular town arranged round the palace and the principal mosque, in the form of a series of concentric walls between which were the houses of private individuals and those belonging to the monarch's favourites. A rampart with 360 towers surrounded the whole thing. Four broad streets ran through the city in the form of a St. Andrew's Cross, and it was entered by four gates each set at an angle, with multiple defences, notably a ditch filled with water brought from the Nahr 'Isa and the Tigris.

This circular city of al-Mansur with its shops housed under arcades along the four converging streets, soon became too small, and lack of space obliged the town to spread in two directions, south towards the suburb of al-Karkh, a trading and craftsman area, and east beyond the river which could be crossed by a pontoon-bridge. It was here, far from the milling crowd, that the residential district grew up, with the caliph's palace, the dar al-Khilafa, as its most important feature. This move to extend the town on the east bank started in 768. Thirty or forty years later, under Harun ar-Rashid and al-Ma'mun, in the early ninth century, Baghdad was a densely populated urban area measuring about 10 kilometres by 9, roughly the same size as Paris within the outer boulevards. It then became the largest city in the world.
—Maurice Lombard, *The Golden Age of Islam* (Princeton: Markus Wiener, 2004), 124–26.

These are the features of the world in which Ibn Fadlan was born and lived. The Islamic religion had not yet been codified or frozen into the formal schools of law, and the seal of finality had not been set upon further thought and development in theology or philosophy. Ibn Fadlan lived in a time when Islamic lands were the most cultured and flourishing in all the world. So he probably felt he was bringing enlightenment, as well as a new faith, to a region of backwardness and even savagery. For Islam, it always has been asserted, is more than a religion, encompassing a way of life and an all-embracing culture.

We do not know the background of Ibn Fadlan, except that he was considered an Arab, learned in the laws and customs of Islam, and a confidant of the Caliph. We know that he was from Baghdad, and in his time Baghdad's population was mainly Muslim and mostly Sunni. The dissent in interpretations of the faith that had characterized the early 'Abbasid Caliphate had subsided, while Islamic mysticism, later organized in Sufi orders, was embryonic. In the Baghdad of Ibn Fadlan, Islam had come to be a multi-ethnic religion with a governing system that tolerated "People of the Book," but that broadly rewarded conversion to Islam.

The geographical dictionary of Yaqut—as well as a much later writer, Amin Razi, who compiled a huge encyclopedia of earlier writers with excerpts of their writings in 1593—give our author's full name as Ahmad ibn Fadlan ibn al-'Abbas ibn Rashid ibn Hammad. He was the client of Muhammad ibn Sulaiman, who was a prominent general of the Caliphal court. In the early days of the Arab conquests, the word "client" (*maula*) meant an auxiliary attached to a Bedouin tribe, but by the tenth century it probably meant that Ibn Fadlan was an assistant or chief scribe to Sulaiman, his patron. The name "Fadlan" probably derives from the Arabic root *fadl,* meaning "to excel or surpass."

The use of the word "sultan" in the text is puzzling, since no such ruler existed in Ibn Fadlan's time. A later hand may have interpolated the word into the original account, after a sultan had come into existence, but the use of the word here could simply mean the government of the Caliphate. Likewise, it is unclear when Ibn Fadlan mentions "the ambassador" whether he means Nadhir al-Hurami or Sausan al-Rasi, a client of

Nadhir's who was one of the members of the embassy. Nadhir may have been responsible for the embassy as well as foreign affairs and protocol at the court of the Caliph. In any case, it is clear that Ibn Fadlan finally became responsible for the success of the embassy, as well as being the person who read the letter of the Caliph to the king of the Bulghars, and who made the record of the trip.

Ibn Fadlan's mission emerged in response to a message from the king of the Bulghars. Who was the king of the Bulghars, and why did he send a message to the Caliph? His full name, it seems, was Almish ibn Shilki Elteber, although the last seems to have been a title. Inasmuch as we have little information about the language of the Volga Bulghars of that time, the meaning of his name is unclear. He ruled a kingdom on the upper Volga River, roughly corresponding to modern Tataristan. His kingdom included many tribes who followed various pagan rites, as well as some Muslim converts, and it is likely that he sought to unite all of them under a single monotheistic faith, and thereby to consolidate his power by creating, in effect, a state religion. Also, since he paid tribute to the Khazars and wished to be free of this dependence, he sought the support of the enemy of the Khazars to the south of their domains—the area ruled by the Caliph. He hardly thought that the Caliph would send an army to assist him, but joint action against the Khazars from the north and south could not be excluded. Almish asked for aid in building a fortress and for instruction in the Islamic religion (to add to what had previously been brought to the Bulghars by Khwarazmian merchants and other Muslims).

The Khazars had split the Bulghars, one group of them going west to the Balkans and the other retreating north on the Volga. The Khazar kingdom had already retreated from the area south of the Caucasus Mountains (present-day Azerbaijan) under pressure from the Caliphate and had established itself as the principal hegemonic nation on the steppes of southern Russia. By the time of Ibn Fadlan, many tribes under Khazar rule had declared their independence or had moved to the west, as the main body of Pechenegs did. So Ibn Fadlan came at a time of a shifting ethnic picture on the steppes. Shortly before this time the Magyars, related to the Volga Bulghars, had moved farther to the west, probably under attack by the Pechenegs. The Volga Bulghars, however, lost their Ugrian language and in time adopted a Turkic tongue, while the Magyars maintained their Ugrian language on the plains of Hungary to the present.

The inhabitants of Baghdad at that time knew little about the north and called the various peoples there "Saqaliba." The origin of this term is uncertain. Some scholars derive the word from the name of the Slavs, or from the common noun "slave," but no agreement exists. Ibn Fadlan was interested in what he saw and heard, as well as eager to instruct the king and his court in Islamic doctrines and practices. The Caliph, for his part, would not have been averse to increasing the *dar al-Islam*, the domain of Islam, since it would give him influence over another potentate, even though the latter was far from Baghdad. Various advantages, such as heightened prestige, gifts and objects of trade, and possibly slaves for his bodyguard, would increase his influence among his own subjects and among all Muslims, wherever they were. So the expenses of an embassy, underwritten by the Caliph, were well worth the results.

CHAPTER II

Central Asian silver plate of the 8th–9th cent.,
similar to Sasanian dishes

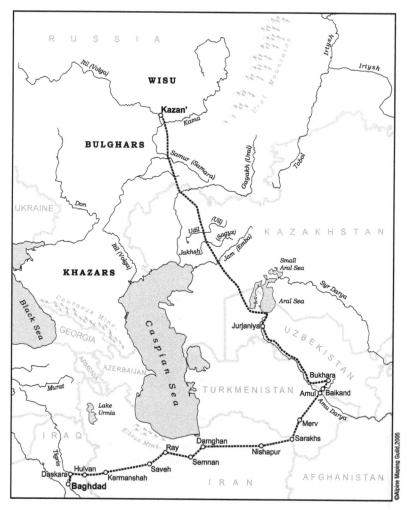

Route of Ibn Fadlan

1:23 Million

| 0 | 150 | 300 Miles |

| 0 | 250 | 500 Km |

His Book and Geography

We know little about Ibn Fadlan except what we can glean from his own story, which does not include much personal information. His account reads like a diary, reporting what he saw, heard, or experienced, plus remarks about his observations. His style is straightforward, without the encomium (flattery of a patron) typical of later literature. Nor is he given to fantastic stories, although his descriptions probably contain some exaggeration. Since his main task was to instruct the king of the Bulghars in the Islamic faith, what he says should be viewed in the context of a pious Muslim scholar from the cosmopolitan capital of Baghdad adventuring on a long and arduous journey into parts little known to his contemporaries.

Nonetheless, there are several questions about his trip that may tentatively be answered. First, why should the Caliphate have dispatched a missionary to the north at this time? And second, why did he make such a wide detour through Central Asia instead of going by the shorter Caucasus route?

The end of the ninth and beginning of the tenth century was a period of intense proselytizing of Islam, in part engendered by the far-reaching activities of heretical Ismaili missionaries of the Fatimid Caliphate in Egypt, rivals to the 'Abbasids in Baghdad. Ibn Fadlan mentions meeting a representative of the Ismaili mission in Damghan, Iran. The competition between these two factions (which later turned deadly under the Assassins, led by Hasan al-Sabah), stirred the Sunni religious establishment to greater efforts in the propagation of their brand of Islam.

This was also a time when many Zoroastrians migrated to India. The end of the tolerant, easy-going atmosphere of the early Caliphate under Ma'mun and Harun al-Rashid, and the beginning of discrimination and pressure for non-Muslims to convert to Islam, most likely drove this migration. Competition between followers of Sunni Islam and the Ismailis, for example, led the inhabitants of the oases of the central deserts of Iran and outlying villages in the mountains, who had hitherto continued to maintain a form of Zoroastrianism, to convert to Islam. The travels of Nasir-e Khusrau, a century later than Ibn Fadlan, reveal the end of a period of conversion after which Islam was triumphant in most of the east, except for pockets of Zoroastrians in villages of Yazd, Kerman, and Fars and in isolated parts of the Zagros and Elburz Mountains.

Ibn Fadlan's group followed an ancient route from the lowlands of Iraq to the Iranian plateau, where the easiest passage was by the town of Hulwan, near present Qasr-e Shirin in Iran.

Winter landscape in northern Iran

The route then passed through Kermanshah, at that time called Qirmisin, climbing higher in the mountains to Hamadan through Sawa (today Saveh) on to Ray south of Tehran. The "district of Ray" implies a different jurisdiction from the town of Ray itself. The journey continued south of mountains through Semnan, Damghan, and Nishapur and then northeast to Sarakhs and Merv, where the Iranian plateau slopes down to the Central Asian lowlands of desert. Then followed the crossing of the Amu Darya to Paikand, a center of commerce, and to Bukhara, where the "Fur Road" branched to Khwarazm and the steppes. Nearing the Ural Mountains, our voyagers deviated from the usual path through the town of Itil (near contemporary Astrakhan) to go far to the north over many rivers to the upper Volga, home of the Bulghars.

Why did they go so far north? Most likely the choice of itinerary was dictated by two factors: the political enmity of the Khazar kingdom in the northern Caucasus, and the availability of caravans on the trade route from Khwarazm in Central Asia to the Volga River in present-day Russia. We do not know what the relations between the Caliphate and the Khazar kingdom were in the year 922, nor is it clear whether Judaism was still prominent among the notables of the Khazars at that time. Although the kingdom was then entering a period of decline, it is nonetheless safe to assume that the route through the Caucasus was not open for an embassy of the Caliph to the king of the Bulghars, since the Khazars hardly could have welcomed an alliance supported by a common religion between their northern and southern neighbors.

The route from Baghdad through Central Asia, on the other hand, followed the age-old "Silk Road," and from Khwarazm an established "Fur Road" to the north. The Silk Road was the main trade route between the Mediterranean and China's rich northern plains. But competition from the "Sea Route" between south Arabia and China's southeast coast had already begun. In the fifteenth century, insecurity caused by Mongol and Timurid tribal movements in Central Asia would interrupt the Silk Road, and this, coupled with the Portuguese circumnavigation of Africa, would bring about the stagnation of the land route.

If we follow the map, the route followed by Ibn Fadlan veered from the usual path only to swing to the east of the Volga River, avoiding the domains of the Khazars. From Khwarazm to Bulghar the journey took two months, although in the spring the melting snows made crossing rivers difficult, as mentioned in the account. Probably his return trip was faster, but we have no information about the time, or any details, of that journey.

What did caravans carry between Khwarazm and the land of the Bulghars, which appears to have been the market center for many peoples of the north? In Central Asia, demand for furs from the north—sable, ermine, mink, marten, fox, and beaver— was high, although in the warm lowlands of Mesopotamia furs were only a luxury or stylish commodity. Amber from the Baltic was sought as a talisman against the evil eye, as well as an orna- ment, and ivory from walruses and narwhals was a prized lux- ury in the Islamic world. Honey, wax, birch bark, and dried fish were also articles of trade from northern regions.

In return, the Ugrian-speaking peoples of northern Russia treasured silver objects from the south. The largest collection of Sasanian and Central Asian silver vessels and plates is in the Hermitage museum of St. Petersburg, most having been unearthed by peasants from the roots of trees where they had been buried. It seems that the Kama River valley people, who offered them to the spirits or deities in the trees, especially ven- erated large trees. Coins from the lands of Islam not only were valued for their silver content but were also used as currency in northern Russia, as we know from the fact that some coins were broken in half or in quarters, signifying use as specie.

International trade was well developed, not only between Central Asia and the north, but also with China and India. We hear a century later of a merchant in Merv who had a warehouse in Bulghar on the Volga and another in Gujarat in India. As mid-

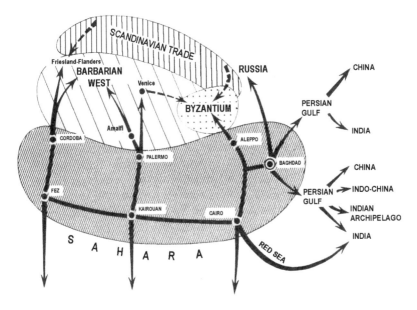

Trading connections of the Muslim World

dlemen in trade between north and south and between east and west, the merchants of Central Asia became wealthy, and in the pre-Mongol period this wealth was the basis of a flowering culture. It is interesting to speculate on whether an incipient middle class of merchants and craftsmen first developed in the oasis states of Central Asia in ancient times, rather than in Iran. Wealth in Iran was primarily in land, and society was divided between the wealthy landholders and the mass of poor peasants. Only at the end of the Sasanian Empire did Iranian merchants achieve a standing comparable to their role in Bukhara and Samarkand.

Geography books in Arabic by Istakhri, Ibn Hauqal, and others give information about local trade between the oasis cities of Central Asia and the Turkic tribes near them. The objects of this trade were more varied than those of international commerce, which was primarily for luxury objects, or at least for valuable

Arabic world map by Istakhri, 10th century

items such as spices. The accounts tell us that tools, bread, household objects such as pots and pans, cloth, rugs, brocades, and dried fruit were traded for sheep and goats, skins, slaves, wool, and leather, although the last was frequently returned in finished objects such as saddles. Thus, it appears that trade was far more important in the oasis towns than it was elsewhere. Khwarazmians dominated the trade with the Turks and with Russia, as the Sogdians did with China.

The Arabs made much use of the Volga waterway, and Norsemen, Russians, Khazars and Arabs met one another along it. For the most part, geographers and cartographers could obtain at first hand the information they needed, for they were travellers too. Al-Mas'udi was a frequent visitor to the Caspian; and Ibn Haukal, whose work, the "Book of Roads and Kingdoms," contained an atlas of Islam, met al-Istakhri during one of his journeys. This is his description of the meeting: "He (Istakhri) showed me the geographical maps in his work, and, when I had commented on them, he gave me his work with the words, 'I can see that you were born under a lucky star, therefore take my work and make such improvements as you think fit'. I took it, altered it in several particulars, and returned it to him."
—Leo Bagrow and R.A. Skelton,
The History of Cartography (Chicago: Precedent, 1985), 56.

There was one other traveler in Inner Asia who left an account of his travels shortly after Ibn Fadlan. Called Abu Dulaf al-Yanbu'i, he wrote an account of a journey to western China, but his work is highly fanciful and indicates that the author only gathered material from elsewhere to embellish the tale of a trip he never made. Otherwise one important book of geography, which has not survived, was compiled by al-Jaihani, the chief minister of the Samanid ruler Nasr ibn Ahmad (914–934). Almost certainly al-Jaihani obtained information about the northern regions from Ibn Fadlan on his return trip, which he included in his book, and which became the main source for information about the pagan world of Inner Asia. The other important books of geography in Arabic (Istakhri, Ibn Hauqal, etc.) were concerned with the Islamic world and give us very little information about the lands and peoples to the north, which is why the account of Ibn Fadlan is important.

The Meshhed manuscript and other accounts of the journey

In 1923 the full account of Ibn Fadlan's trip from Baghdad to Bulghar was discovered in the town of Meshhed. Before the discovery of this manuscript—which was a collection of geographical texts, including tracts by Abu Dulaf and Ibn Faqih—our information was derived from scattered notices in the geographical dictionary of Yaqut, and a few remarks in Ahmad Tusi, both compiled almost two centuries after Ibn Fadlan's travels. Tusi dedicated his work to a Seljuk ruler, Toghrul ibn Arslan, who ruled from 1173 to 1193 (Togan 1939, xi). Amin Razi, an author who wrote in Persian and flourished circa 1593, also has excerpts from Ibn Fadlan, but no additions to what we already have may be found in his work entitled *Haft Iqlim*. Zeki-Velidi Togan (1939) published the Meshhed manuscript portion of Ibn Fadlan's travels with a German translation, while a facsimile of the manuscript with a Russian translation was published by A. P. Kovalevskii (1939). Marius Canard (1958) later made a French translation, in which he added excerpts from Yaqut.

The text of the Meshhed manuscript is clearly an epitome of a fuller account, and whoever made the abbreviation seems to have been interested mostly in the descriptions of the Turks in the regions to the north of Khwarazm and in that part of the journey. But we cannot be sure whether the Meshhed manuscript is defective, or whether only part of the trip has been preserved. It is probably useless to speculate on the purpose of the epitome, who ordered it to be compiled, or to whom it was dedicated. The manuscript is old, dating from perhaps a century, more or less, after Ibn Fadlan's voyage. If it were compiled for a later Turkic ruler, then the emphasis on the early part of his travels in the land of the Turks would be understandable.

It should be noted that Togan, who had been one of the leaders of the short-lived Bashkirt republic in 1917, was arrested and condemned to death after the Bolsheviks came to power. His colleagues freed him from prison and he fled to Central Asia, where he aided local forces in their struggle against the Communists. Again forced to flee in 1923 when the Red Army overran all of Central Asia, he ended up in Iranian territory, and in Meshhed he heard about the library at the shrine of Imam Reza. Since he was a Muslim, he was permitted to enter and read in the library of the shrine. He copied much of the manuscript, including the treatise of Ibn Fadlan, and this became his doctoral dissertation in Bonn University, where he taught from 1931 to 1935. According to Hellmut Ritter (1942, 98) Ernst Herzfeld made photographs of the Meshhed manuscript and deposited them in the Prussian State Library in Berlin, and Togan made use of these to complete his copy. Togan later became a professor in Bonn. In 1939 he went to Turkey to became professor of Turkic history in Istanbul University.

In 1935, after learning of the existence of the manuscript, the Soviet Academy of Sciences requested a copy of Ibn Fadlan from the Iranian government, which was duly sent and became the basis of the edition by A.P. Kovalevskii in 1939. Kovalevskii had succumbed to the Stalinist purges by 1939 and his name does not appear anywhere in the book, since at the time he was under arrest. Thus, the German edition of Ibn Fadlan, with printed text, appeared several months earlier than the Russian edition with its facsimile. The notes to both for the most part are similar, except where identifications of rivers in Russia are different because of differing views of his route. Both remain standard editions of the Meshhed text.

CHAPTER III

Late-nineteenth-century print of Kirghiz costumes in Siberia

Translation of His Travels

This is [the book of Ahmad ibn Fadlan al-'Abbas ibn Rashid ibn Hammad, a client of Muhammad ibn Sulaiman, the ambassador from al-Muqtadir to the king of the Saqaliba] in which he recounts what he saw in the land[s] of the Turks, the Khazars, the Rus, the Saqaliba, the Bashkirs and others, of the many types of their religion, of the histories of their kings, and [of] the way they act in many affairs of their life.

Ahmad ibn Fadlan says: The letter of Almish ibn Shilki, the Yiltawar [Elteber], the King of the Saqaliba, reached the Commander of the Faithful, al-Muqtadir; he asked him therein to send someone who would instruct him in religion and make him acquainted with the laws of Islam, [and] who would build for him a mosque and erect for him a pulpit mentioning his name, from which might be carried out the mission of converting his people in his whole country, and in all the districts of his kingdom. And he prayed the Caliph to build a fortress wherein he might defend himself against hostile kings. The intermediary in this matter was Nadhir al-Hurami. Everything that was asked for was granted him.

I was chosen to read the message of the Caliph to him, to hand over what he had sent him as gifts, and to have oversight over those learned in the law and the teachers. To carry the expenses in constructing what we have mentioned, and for pay-

---

This is my old translation of the first part of the trip, until reaching the Bulghars, taken from "Notes on the Risala of Ibn Fadlan" (Blake and Frye 1949).

ment to the learned in law and the teachers, there were applied the revenues of one of the estates of Ibn al-Furat, that which is known as the estate of Artakhushmitan, in the land of Khwarazm. The ambassador of the ruler of the Saqaliba to Muqtadir was a man who was called 'Abdallah ibn Bashtu al-Khazari, and the ambassador of the sultan was Sausan al-Rasi, the client of Nadhir al-Hurami. Also there were Tekin al-Turki, Bars al-Saqlabi, and I too was with them, as I have said. The gifts for him, for his wife, his children, his brothers, and his generals, and at the same time the drugs for which he had written to Nadhir, were all handed over to him.

So we started on Thursday, the 11th of Safar of the year 309 [June 21, 921] from the City of Peace [Baghdad]. We stopped a day in Nahrawan and from there went swiftly on until we reached Daskara, where we stopped for three days. Then we traveled straight onward without any detours until we reached Hulwan. There we stayed two days. From there we went to Qirmisin, where we remained two days. Then we started and traveled until we reached Hamadan, where we remained three days. Then we went further to Sawa where we remained two days. From there we came to Ray where we remained eleven days, waiting for Ahmad ibn 'Ali the brother of Sa'luk, because he was in the district of Ray. Then we went to the district of Ray and remained there three days.

Then we sent off for Semnan, from thence to Damghan and met there Ibn Qarin, the representative of the Da'i [Ismaili mission]. We mingled [in hiding] with a caravan and went swiftly to Nishapur, where Laila ibn Nu'man had just been killed, and we found there the army commander of Khurasan, Humuwayh Kusa. Then we went to Sarakhs and Merv and from there to Qushmahan, which lies at the edge of the desert of Amul, and remained here three days, letting the camels rest so that we could enter the sand-steppe.

Afterwards we came across the sand-steppe to Amul and crossed the Jaihun [Amu Darya]. Then we came to Afribar, the

Ruins of Bukhara city wall

burg of Tahir ibn 'Ali. We continued to Baikand and then entered into Bukhara. There we paid a visit to the chancellor of the governor of Khurasan, al-Jaihani, whom people in Khurasan call "the elder bulwark." He moved at once to obtain quarters for us and appointed a man to look after our needs, and in general to satisfy any desires we had. After staying in Bukhara several days, he obtained for us an audience with the governor Nasr ibn Ahmad (914–943). We came before him; he was a beardless youth; we greeted him like an *amir* and he bade us to be seated. His talk with us began with the following words: "How did you leave my master, the Commander of the Faithful? May God grant to him, to his guard and to his clients long life and good health." We answered," He is in good health." He said, "May God give him fortune in this regard."

Then the letter from the Caliph was read to him, concerning the transfer of the estate of Artakhushmitan from the Christian al-Fadl ibn Musa, the bailiff of Ibn al-Furat, to the Khwarazmian Ahmad ibn Musa, and that he should send us along with a letter to his governor in Khwarazm so that he should not delay us, and a letter for the [official at the] Turkish gateway to give us an escort and to remove hindrances.

Then he asked, "Where is this Ahmad ibn Musa?" We answered: "We have left him in the City of Peace to follow us within five days." He said: "[I give] obedience and submission to what my master, the Commander of the Faithful, commands, may God lengthen his life."

He says: In the meantime the report had reached the Christian al-Fadl ibn Musa, the bailiff of Ibn al-Furat, and he began to lay traps for Ahmad ibn Musa, and wrote to the heads of police of the towns on the road to Khurasan from the military district of Sarakhs to Baikand, "Keep an eye out for the Khwarazmian Ahmad at the relay points and at the police stations. He is a person of such outward appearance and demeanor. Whoever meets him let him detain him until our letter comes to him, and treat him in accordance with his rank." And so he was arrested at Merv and put in jail. We waited in Bukhara twenty-eight days, and al-Fadl ibn Musa talked it over with 'Abdallah ibn Bashtu and others of our comrades, who began to say: "If we remain here winter will set in, and then we shall not be able to proceed. Ahmad ibn Musa can, however, join us if he follows after us."

I found different kinds of dirhams in Bukhara, one of which was called Ghitrifi, made of copper, fool's gold, and brass. They are accepted without being weighed, but one hundred of them for a silver dirham. In regard to the practice of dowries of their women, it is such: so-and-so son of someone married someone, the daughter of so-and so, for so many thousand Ghitrifi dirhams. Also they use these [dirhams] for the purchase of real estate and slaves. These are the only dirhams they employ. There are other dirhams minted only in brass, and these are forty for a dang. They also have dirhams called Samarkandi, six to a dang.

When I heard the words of 'Abdallah ibn Bashtu and the others, warning of the coming of winter, we left Bukhara, and returned to the river [Jaihun], where we hired a boat for Khwarazm. It was more than two hundred farsakhs from where we obtained the boat to Khwarazm. We only traveled part of the day, and not the entire day because of the cold, until we reached Khwarazm. We had an audience with the governor, Muhammad ibn 'Iraq Khwarazmshah, who showed us honor and a friendly reception, providing us a house.

Three days later he brought us into his presence and counseled us about entering the land of the Turks. He said, "I will not allow you to do that, for it is unlawful for me to permit you to risk your lives, since I know that this is a ruse made by this youth," meaning Tekin. "For he was [formerly] with us as an ironsmith, well acquainted with the selling of iron in the land of the infidels. He is the one who deceived Nadhir and persuaded him to speak to the Caliph, and to deliver to him the letter of the king of the Saqaliba. For the most exalted *amir*, that is the *amir* of Khurasan [Nasr ibn Ahmad, the Samanid] has more right, if it were possible, to initiate a [missionary] embassy in this land [Bulghar] in the name of the Commander of the Faithful. Furthermore, between you and the mentioned land there are a thousand tribes of unbelievers; this [undertaking] is an attempt to deceive the Caliph. That is why I have advised you. So it is necessary to write a letter to the exalted amir that he consult in writing the Caliph, may God strengthen him. Meanwhile you should remain here until an answer comes."

On that day we departed from him. Afterwards we returned to him, remaining respectful and continuing to flatter him and saying, "This is the letter of the Commander of the Faithful; what reason is there to turn again to him in the same [matter]?" Finally he permitted us to go. We went from Khwarazm on the river to Jurjaniya, a distance of fifty *farsakhs* on water from Khwarazm.

I found the debased underweight *dirhams* of Khwarazm struck in lead and brass. They call the *dirham* Taziya, which is four and a half *dangs* by weight. Their moneychangers also sell dice [and toy] tops, as well as *dirhams.*

They are the most vulgar of people in speech and by nature. Their speech is mostly like the chatter of starlings. In this region

there is a village, a day's journey [from Jurjaniya] called Ard-
kwa, the inhabitants of which are called Ardakiwa. Their tongue
is mostly like the croaking of frogs. At the end of every prayer
they curse the Commander of the Faithful, 'Ali ibn Abi Talib,
may God be please with him.

We remained in Jurjaniya several days and the river Jaihun
froze from it source to its end, and the ice was seventeen spans
thick. Horses, mules, donkeys and wagons go over the ice in the
same manner in which they go on roads, the ice being firm and
not giving way. It remains that way for three months, and we
saw the land, which seemed to us as though the gate of bitter
cold had been opened. Snow only falls when there is a strong
and violent wind. When a man wishes to honor another of this
land and show him kindness, he says to him, "Come to me for
conversation, for I have a pleasant fire." He does this when he
especially wants to be considerate and show [his guest] special
favor. However, God the exalted has been kind to them regarding firewood, for he has made it cheap for them. A wagonload
of tamarisk wood, which amounts to about three thousand *ratls,*
can be obtained for two of their *dirhams.*

The custom of their beggars is such that the beggar does not
stand at the door, but enters the house of one of them, where he
sits by the fire for an hour warming himself. Then he says
pekend, which means bread. If he is given some he takes it, if not
he leaves.

Our stay in Jurjaniya was lengthy; that is, we stayed there
some days of the month of Rajab and during the whole of
Sha'aban, Ramadan, and Shawwal. Our long stay was brought
about by the cold and its bitterness. Verily they told me that two
men took twelve camels into one of the bottoms to get wood.
They forgot, however, to take flint and tinder with them, hence
slept in the night without a fire. When they got up the next
morning they found that all the camels had been frozen stiff
from the cold. Verily I beheld that the market place and the
streets were completely empty because of the cold. One could

stroll through most of the streets and market places without meeting anyone or without anyone meeting him. Once as I came out from the bath, and when I came into the house and looked at my beard, I saw it was a lump of ice, so that I had to thaw it out before the fire. I stayed night and day in a house, which was inside another house, and in which a Turkish felt tent was pitched, and I myself was wrapped up in clothes and fur rugs, but in spite of this my cheeks often stuck to the cushion. I also beheld that the water skins in this country, lest they break and be split because of the cold, are wrapped around with sheepskin rugs, but this was of no avail. I saw that the earth, because of the extremity of the cold, formed great clefts, and that a large and ancient tree would split into two halves from this.

About the middle of Shawwal of the year 309 [February 922] the weather began to change. The river Jaihun thawed and we got ourselves the necessary things for the journey. We bought Turkish camels and had made, in view of the rivers we would have to cross in the land of the Turks, skin boats out of camel hides. We laid in a supply of bread, millet, and salted meat for three months. Our acquaintances among the inhabitants of the town directed us in laying in garments, as much as was needed.

Caravan in Central Asia

They depicted the matter in fearful colors and exaggerated the matter. When we underwent this, it was far greater than what had been told to us. Each of us put on a jacket, over that a coat, over that a *pustin* [sheepskin], over that a felt mantle and a helmet of felt, out of which only the two eyes could look, a simple pair of under-drawers and a lined pair, trousers over them, and slippers of leather and over these another pair of boots. When one of us got on a camel, he could not move because of his clothes.

The doctor of law and the teacher and the pages who traveled with us from Baghdad parted from us, fearing to enter this country, so the ambassador, his brother-in-law, two pages, Tekin and Bars, and I proceeded. On the day we had fixed for departure, I said to them: "O people, the page of the king of the Saqaliba is in your train. He has learned about all your affairs and the letters of the sultan [Caliph], which you have, and I have no doubt that the dispatch of 4,000 Musayyabi *dinars* is mentioned in it. You are going to a foreign king; he will demand this money of you." To this they replied: "Have no fear. He will be far from demanding it of us." Then I warned them again and said: "But I know he will demand it of you," but they did not agree.

The caravan was ready to start. We took into our service a guide from the inhabitants of Jurjaniya, whose name was Qlawus. Then trusting in the all-powerful and exalted God, and entrusting our fate to him, we started on Monday the third of Dhulqa'da of the year 309 [March 3, 922] from Jurjaniya. This day we stopped at the burg called Zanjan, that is, [by] the gateway to the Turks. The next morning early we proceeded and halted at a station called Jit. There so much snow fell upon us that the camels plunged in it up to their knees; hence we remained in this station two days. Then we sped straight on into the land of the Turks without taking precautions, and without meeting anyone in the barren and flat steppe. We thus rode ten days meeting with many obstacles and difficulties, bitter cold and unbroken snow storms, in comparison with which the cold in Khwarazm seemed like a summer day, so we forgot all our previous discomforts and were about at the point of giving up the ghost.

One day when we underwent most savage cold, Tekin, who was riding next to me, and along with him one of the Turks, was talking to him in Turkish. Tekin laughed and said to me: "This Turk says to me, 'What will our Lord have of us? He is killing us with cold. If we knew what he wanted we would let him have it.' Then I said: 'Tell him He only wishes of you that you should say: "There is no God save Allah."' The Turk laughed and answered: 'If we knew it we should.'"

Then we came to a place where there was a large quantity of tamarisk wood, and we halted in it. The caravan [people] lit fires, warmed themselves, took off their clothes and spread them out to dry.

Then we set out again and rode every day from midnight until the time of afternoon prayer [hastening more from midday on], covering the greatest distance, and then we halted. When we had ridden fifteen nights in this manner, we arrived at a large mountain where there were many great rocks. There are springs there which jet out from the rocks and the water stays in pools.

After we had crossed, we reached a Turkish tribe, which are called Oghuz. They are nomads and have houses of felt. They stay for a time in one place and then travel on. One sees their dwellings placed here and there according to nomad custom. Although they lead a hard existence they are like asses gone astray. They have no religious bonds with God, nor do they have recourse to reason. They never pray, rather do they call their headmen lords. When one of them takes counsel with his chief about something he says: "O lord, what shall I do in this or the other matter?" Their undertakings are based upon counsel solely among themselves; when they come to an agreement on a matter and have decided to put it through, there comes one of the lowest and basest of them and disrupts their decision.

I have heard how they enounce: "There is no God but Allah

and Muhammad is the prophet of Allah," so as to get close to any Muslims who come to them by these words, but not because they believe them. When one of them has been dealt with unjustly, or something happens to him which he cannot endure, he looks up to the sky and says: "*bir tengri*," that is in Turkish, "By the one God," because *bir* means one in Turkish and *tengri* is in the speech of the Turks God. The Oghuz do not wash themselves either after defecation or urination, nor do they bathe after seminal pollution, or on other occasions. They have nothing whatever to do with water, especially in winter.

Their women do not veil themselves neither in the presence of their own men nor of others, nor does any woman cover any of her bodily parts in the presence of any person. One day we stopped off with one of them and were seated there. The man's wife was present. As we conversed, the woman uncovered her pudendum and scratched it, and we saw her doing it. Then we veiled our faces and said: "I beg God's pardon." Her husband laughed and said to the interpreter: "Tell them she uncovers it in your presence so that you may see it and be abashed, but it is not to be attained. This, however, is better than when you cover it up and yet it is reachable."

Adultery is unknown among them; but whomsoever they find by his conduct that he is an adulterer, they tear him in two. This comes about so: they bring together the branches of two trees, tie him to the branches and then let both trees go and so the man who was tied to the branches is torn in two.

One of them said he heard [my recitation] from the Quran and found that this recitation was beautiful; he approached addressing the interpreter: "Tell him do not stop." One day this man said to me through the interpreter: "Ask this Arab if our God, mighty and glorious, has a wife?" I felt this an enormity and uttered the formulas: "Praise God" and "I beg God's pardon." And he praised God and begged forgiveness, as I had done. This was the custom of the Turks: every time when a Turk hears a Muslim [pronounce these formulas] he repeats them after him.

Their marriage customs are as follows: one of them asks for the hand of a female of another's family, whether his daughter or his sister or any other one of those over whom he has power, against so and so many garments from Khwarazm. When he pays it he brings her home. The marriage price often consists of camels, pack animals, or other things; and no one can take a wife until he has fulfilled the obligation on which he has come to an understanding with those who have power over her in regard to him. If, however, he has met it, then he comes with any ado, enters the abode where she is, [and] takes her in the presence of her father, mother, and brothers; these do not prevent him. If a man dies who has a wife and children, then the eldest of his sons takes her to wife if she is not his mother.

None of the merchants or other Muslims may perform in their presence the ablution after seminal pollution, except in the night when they do not see it, for they get angry and say: "This man wishes to put a spell on us for he is immersing himself in water," and they compel him to pay a fine.

None of the Muslims can enter their country until one of them has become his host, with whom he stays and for whom he brings garments from the lands of Islam and for his wife a kerchief and some pepper, millet, raisins, and nuts. When the Muslim comes to his friend, the latter pitches a tent for him and brings him sheep in accordance with his [the Turk's] wealth, so that the Muslim himself may slaughter the sheep, for the Turks do not slaughter, but one of them beats the sheep on the head until it is dead.

Should any of the Muslims wish to travel further and aught happen to some of his camels and horses, or if he needs resources, he leaves those [incapacitated] with his Turkish friend, takes from him camels, pack animals, and provisions, as much as he needs, and travels further. When he returns from where he went, he pays him [the Turk] money, and gives back his camels and pack animals. And in the same way, when a man stops off with a Turk whom he does not know, and he says to the

Turk: "I am thy guest and I will have some of thy camels, [thy] horses, and thy *dirhams*," he gives him what he wishes. If the merchant dies in that region and the caravan returns, the Turk goes to meet them and says: "Where is my guest?" If they say: "He has died," then he stops the caravan and goes to the most prominent merchant whom he sees among the Muslims, opens his bales while he is looking, and takes of his *dirhams*, just the amount that he had claim upon the [deceased] merchant, without taking a grain more. In the same way, he takes some of the pack animals and camels and he [the Turk] says, "That one [the deceased] was thy cousin; thou art chiefly obligated to pay his debts." And if the [first merchant] has fled, the Turk does the same thing and tells him: "He is a Muslim just as thou art. You take from him." If he does not encounter his Muslim guest on the caravan trail, then he asks another [or a third] one: "Where is he?" If he receives an indication, he sets out to find him, journeying for days until he reaches him, and takes away from him what he had of his property and also what he has presented to the [Muslim].

Also the following is a custom of the Turks. When he comes to Jurjaniya, he asks for his host and stays with him until he leaves. If, however, the Turk dies at his Muslim host's house, and if a caravan is traveling through, and his Muslim host is with it, the Turks kill him, saying, "Thou hast killed him in thy prison. Hadst thou not imprisoned him, he would not have died." In the same way when the Muslim has the Turk drink strong drink, so that the Turk falls off a wall, they kill him for this reason. In case the Muslim host is not found in the caravan, they set upon the most prominent among them and kill him.

The Turks count the custom of pederasty as a terrible sin. There once came a man of the inhabitants of Khwarazm to stay with the clan of the Kudarkin, the viceroy of the Turkish king. He stayed with his host for a time to buy sheep. The Turk had a beardless son, and the Khwarazmian sought unceasingly to lead him astray until he got him to consent to his will. In the meantime the Turk came in and caught them in *flagrante delicto*. Then the Turk brought up the matter before the Kudarkin and said to him: "Assemble the Turks." The Kudarkin assembled them; once they had gathered he said to the Turk: "Does thou wish that I pass a just or unjust sentence?" The Turk said: "According to justice." He said: "Bring thy son here." He brought him. He said: "The verdict is he and the merchant should be killed together." The Turk was appalled because of this and said: "I will not give up my son." Thereupon the Kudarkin said: "Then the merchant may ransom himself." He did it and paid the Turk for what he had done to his son with sheep and presented the Kudarkin with 400 sheep because he had saved him, and left the land of the Turks.

The first of the rulers and chiefs whom we met was the little Yanal. He had become a convert to Islam, but they told him: "If thou acceptest Islam, then thou canst not be our chieftain." So he renounced Islam. When we got to the place where he was, he told us: "I shall not permit you to pass, because verily this is something that we have not heard of, and concerning which we never believed that it could be." We acted in a friendly manner with him until he gave in for a jacket from Jurjaniya worth ten *dirhams*, a piece of cloth, some loaves of bread, a handful of raisins, and a hundred nuts. When we had given him this, he made obeisance. That is their custom; when one man honors another, he makes obeisance before him. Then the Yanal said: "If my houses were not off the road, I would have brought you sheep and unground grain." Then he departed from us and we traveled on further.

The next morning one of the Turks met us. He was ugly in figure, dirty in appearance, despicable in manner, and base in nature. We had entered into a heavy rain. Then he said: "Halt." Then the whole caravan halted, which consisted of 3,000 animals and 5,000 men. Then he said: "No single one of you may proceed." We halted then in obedience to his command. Then we said to him: "We are friends of the Kudarkin." He began to

laugh and said: "Who is the Kudarkin? I defecate on his beard."
Then he said *pekend* that is bread in the language of Khwarazm.
Then I gave him a few sheets of bread. He took them and said:
"You may go further. I take pity on you."

He [Ibn Fadlan] says: If any [of the Turks] becomes sick and
has female and male slaves, these look after him and no one of
his family comes near him. They pitch a tent for him apart from
the houses, and he does not depart from it until he dies or gets
well. If, however, he is a slave or poor man, they leave him in the
desert and go on their way.

When one of their [prominent] men dies, they dig for him a
large pit in the form of a house, and they go to him, dress him
in a robe with his belt and bow, put a drinking cup of wood in
his hand with intoxicating drink in it, and place in front of him
a wooden vessel of mead. They come with his entire possessions

Turkish gravestone

and put them with him in this house. Then they set him down
in it. They then build a structure over him and make a kind of
cupola out of mud. Then they go at his horses, and in accordance with their number they slaughter one to two hundred at
the grave down to the last one. Then they eat their flesh down
to the head, the hooves, the hide, and the tail, for they hang
these upon wooden poles and say: "These are his steeds on
which he rides to paradise." If he has killed any one and has
been a hero, then they carve statues out of wood in the number
of those whom he has slain, place them on his grave and say:
"These are his pages that serve him in paradise." Sometimes
they delay slaughtering the animals for a day or two, and then
an old man from among their great ones stirs them up and says:
"I have seen N.N., that is, the dead man, in my sleep and he said
to me: 'Here thou seest me. My comrades have overtaken me
and my feet were too weak to follow them. I cannot overtake
them and so have remained alone.'" In this case the people go at
his steeds, kill them, and hang them up on his grave. After a day
or two the same elder comes to them and says: "I have seen
N.N. [in a dream] and he said, 'Inform my family and my comrades that I have overtaken those who have gone before me, and
I have recovered from my toil.'"

He [Ibn Fadlan] says: All the Turks pluck their beards with
exception of their moustaches. I once saw one of their old men
who had pulled his beard out and only left a little of it under his
chin, and had wrapped a fleece around so that when one looked
at him from a distance, one could not doubt that it was a goat.

The ruler of the Oghuz is called *yabghu*. That is the name of
the ruler and everyone who rules over this tribe bears this name.
His subordinate is called Kudarkin and so each subordinate to a
chieftain is called Kudarkin.

After leaving their district we stopped with their army commander whose name was Etrek ibn al-Qataghan. He pitched
Turkish tents for us and had us stay in them. He himself had a
large establishment, servants and large dwellings. He drove in

sheep for us that we might slaughter them, and put horses at our disposal for riding. He invited a crowd of his family and relatives and killed for them many sheep.

We had given them gifts of garments, raisins, nuts, pepper, and millet. I noticed the wife, who had been the wife of his father, take meat, sour milk, and something of what we had bestowed upon her and go out from the dwelling into the desert. She dug a little trench and buried in it that which she had with her and muttered some words. I asked the interpreter: "What is she saying?" He answered: "She says that this is a gift for al-Qataghan, the father of Etrek, which the Arabs had given to him."

In the evening I went with an interpreter to the chieftain while he was sitting in his tent. We had with us the letter of Nadhir al-Hurami to him, in which he proposed to him [conversion] to Islam, and spoke glowingly of it to him. He also sent him fifty *dinars*, among which were a number of Musayyabi *dinars*, and further three *mitqals* of musk, [pieces of] red leather, [and] two bolts of cloth from Merv, out of which we cut two jackets for him. Then came a pair of boots of red leather, a coat of brocade, and five coats of silk. We handed him his gifts and presented his wife as well with a head shawl and a ring. Then I read him the letter. He said to the interpreter: "I will give you no answer until you return, and then I will write the sultan [Caliph] what my decision is." Then he took of the coat of brocade, which he wore to don the garment of honor we have mentioned. Then I saw that the jacket which he had underneath was fraying apart from dirt, for it is their custom that no one shall take off the garment which he wears on his body until it disintegrates. Verily he pulled out his entire beard and his moustache, so that he looked like a eunuch.

And I have observed that the Turks spoke of him as their best horseman; and I in very truth saw one day when he raced with us on his horse, and as a goose flew over us, how he strung his bow and then guiding his horse under it, shot at it and brought it down.

One day he sent for the leaders who were close to him, that

is the Tarkhan, the Yanal, the son of their brother, and Yglz [Yughrush?]. The Tarkhan was the most prominent and influential among them; he was crippled and blind and had a maimed hand. Thereupon he [Etrek] said to them: "These are the messengers of the king of the Arabs to my relative Almish ibn Shilki, and I should not let them pass without taking counsel with you." Then the Tarkhan spoke: "This is a matter that we have never yet seen and of which we have never yet heard. Never has the ambassador of the sultan [Caliph] traveled through [our country] since our ancestors and we have been here. My feeling is that the sultan is playing us a trick; these he has really sent to the Khazars to stir them up against us. The best is to hew the ambassadors in twain and we shall take all that they have with them."

Another of them said: "No, we should rather take what they have with them and leave them naked so that they may return thither whence they came." Another said: "No, we have captives with the king of the Khazars, so we ought to send these to ransom them." They kept discussing these matters among themselves for seven days, while we were in a situation similar to death, until they agreed to open the road and let us pass. We presented the Tarkhan with a garment of honor, two jackets from Merv and two pieces of textiles, and to his comrades each a robe and the same to the Yanal. We gave them pepper, millet, and some sheets of bread and they departed from us.

And we traveled forth until we came to the river Yaghindi. There the men took their skin boats that had been made from camel's hide, spread them out, and took the goods from the Turkish camels; and as the boats are round, they put the goods inside them until they spread out. Then they filled them up full with garments and wares. When each skin boat was full, a group of five, six, or four men, more or less, sat in them. They took in their hands birch wood and used it like oars, and kept on rowing while the water carried the boat on, and it spun around until we got across. With regard to the horses and camels, they called to them and they came swimming across. And it is absolutely necessary that first of all a group of warriors with weapons should be transported across to form a vanguard for the people and a rearguard against the Bashkirs, lest these make an attack upon the people as they cross.

So we crossed the river Yaghindi as we have described. Then we crossed a river called the Jam also on the same skin boats. Then we crossed the river Jakhish, then the Udil, then the Ardin, then the Warish, the Akhati, then the Ubna; all these are large rivers.

Then we arrived at the Pechenegs. These had encamped by a still lake like the sea. They were dark brown [and] powerful and they shaved their beards. They were poor in contrast to the Oghuz, for I saw people among the Oghuz who possessed 10,000 horses and 100,000 sheep. What the sheep mostly eat is the grass, which is found under the snow. They paw with their hooves to seek the grass, and when they do not find it they eat the snow and become extraordinarily fat. When the summer comes and they eat grass, then they get thinner. We remained a day with the Pechenegs.

Then we started out and came to the river Jayikh; this is the largest and swiftest flowing that we saw. Verily I saw how a skin boat upset in it, so that those who were on it were drowned. Some from the company perished and a number of the camels and horses drowned. We crossed this river only with difficulty. Then we went a few days further and crossed the river Jakha, then the river Azhin, then the Bajagh, then the Samur, then the Kinal, then the Sukh, and then the river Kunjulu.

We halted in the country of a tribe of Turks called the Bashkirs, and we were extremely wary of them, for they are the most wicked of the Turks, the dirtiest of them, and the most audacious in the commission of murder. Thus when one man meets another, he cuts off his head, takes it with him, and leaves the body. They shave off their beards and eat lice. One of them will examine the seam of his tunic and grind the lice with his teeth. One of them who had accepted Islam was with us and used to serve us. I saw him find a louse in his clothing. He crushed it between his fingernails and licked it, and he said when he saw me: "Good."

Each of them sculpts a piece of wood the size of a phallus and hangs it on himself. If he is about to take a trip or to meet an enemy, he kisses it and prostrates himself before it saying: "O my Lord, do unto me such and such." I said to the interpreter: "Ask one of them as to their justification for this, and as to why he believes it to be his lord." He said: "I came out of something similar to this, and I do not know any creator of myself other than it."

Among them are those who maintain that they have twelve lords: a lord for the winter; a lord for the summer; a lord for rain; a lord for the wind; a lord for trees; a lord for horses; a lord for water; a lord for the night; a lord for the day; a lord for death; and a lord for the earth. The lord who is in heaven is the greatest of them all, although he is in complete agreement with the others. Each of them approves of what his partner does. May God be greatly exalted above all that the iniquitous say.

We saw a group of them who worship snakes, a group who worship fish, and a group who worship cranes. They informed me that they were once engaged in a battle with a group of their enemies who had put them to flight, when the cranes let out a cry behind them, and they became frightened and fled, after first having routed them. For this reason they came to worship the cranes. They said, "This is our lord and these are his actions. He put our enemies to flight." And they worship them for this reason.

Then we left the land of the Bashkirs and crossed the river Jaramshan, then the river Uran, then the river Uram, the river Baynakh, the river Watigh, then Niyasnah, then Jaushir [or Jaushiz]. Between each of the rivers we have mentioned, the distance is a journey of two, three, [or] four days, more or less.

When we were at a distance of a day's and a night's journey

from the king of the Saqaliba, who is the person we had come to see, he dispatched the four rulers who were subject to his authority, as well as his brothers and his sons, to meet us. They brought with them bread, meat, and millet, and [they] rode along with us.

When we were two *farsakhs* distant from him [the king], he came to meet us himself. When he saw us he dismounted and prostrated himself, giving thanks to God, might and majesty be His. He carried money in his sleeve, which he showered upon us. He pitched tents for us and we settled ourselves in them.

Our arrival was on Sunday, the twelfth of Muharram in the year 310 [May 12, 922]. The distance from Jurjaniya to his town was seventy days. We remained Sunday, Monday, Tuesday, and Wednesday in the tents that had been set up for us, until he had assembled the rulers, the commanders, and the people of his country to hear the reading of the [Caliph's] letter.

When it was Thursday, and they had assembled, we unfurled the two standards that were with us, saddled the horse with the saddle that had been sent to him, clothed the king in black, and made him don a turban. I brought out the [Caliph's] letter and said to him: "It is not permitted for us to remain seated while the letter is being read." He rose to his feet, as did all those who were present among the notables of his kingdom. He was a very stout and paunchy man.

I began and read the preamble of the letter. When I reached the part that says: "Peace be upon you! I address myself to you in rendering praise unto God, other than whom there is no deity," I said: "Return the greeting to the Commander of the Faithful." He returned the salutation, and all of them to a man returned it. The interpreter continued to translate for us [the letter] word for word. When we had finished reading it, they shouted the magnification of God in such a manner that the earth trembled.

I then read the letter of the vizier, Hamid ibn al-'Abbas, while he remained standing. I then bid him be seated, and he sat down while the letter of Nadhir al-Hurami was being read. When I had finished it his companions showered a large amount of money on him. I then took out the gifts of perfume, clothing, and pearls for him and his wife. I continued to display the gifts before him and her item by item until we were done.

I then, in the presence of the people, bestowed upon his wife a robe of honor as she sat by his side, this being their custom and usage. When I had bestowed upon her the robe of honor, the women showered money upon her. And we departed.

After an hour had elapsed, he sent for us, and we went before him as he sat in his tent with the rulers on his right side. He then bid us be seated on his left-hand side. We found his sons sitting in front of him, while he sat alone upon a throne covered with Greek brocade. He called for a table and it was brought, and on it was only roast meat.

He himself began, took a knife, cut off a bite-size morsel and ate it, then a second and a third. Then he cut off a piece and gave it to Sausan the ambassador. As the latter took it, a small table was brought and placed in front of him. Such is the custom; no one extends his hand to the food until the king gives him a bite, and as soon as he takes it, a table is brought to him. He offered me a bite and a table was brought to me. He then cut a piece and offered it to the ruler who was on his right, and a table was brought to him. He then served the second ruler and a table was brought to him. Then he served the fourth ruler, and a table was brought to him. He then served his sons, and tables were brought to them.

We ate, each one from his own table, no one sharing it with him, and no one taking anything from a table other than his own. When the meal was over, each one of them carried to his house whatever was left on his table.

When we had eaten, he called for a beverage made from honey, which they call *suju*, which takes a day and a night to prepare. He drank a cup, then rose to his feet and said: "This is [an expression] of my pleasure with my master, the Commander of the Faithful, may God prolong his life." The four rulers and his sons stood up when he stood up, as we did. He did that repeatedly, until he had done it three times. We then departed from his presence.

The *khutba* [invocation] used to be read for him from his pulpit prior to my arrival, in the following manner: "O God, prosper King Yiltawar, King of the Bulghars." I said to him, "Verily God is the King, and no one but He, majesty and might be His, should be called by this name from the pulpit. Behold your master, the Commander of the Faithful. He has been content to have himself referred to from his pulpits in the East and West in the following manner: 'O God, prosper your servant and your vicar, Ja'far the *imam*, al-Muqtadir bi'llah, the Commander of the Faithful.' And so it was with his forefathers, the caliphs before him. The Prophet, may God bless and grant him peace, said: 'Do not praise me as the Christians have praised Jesus, son of Mary, for I am but the servant of God and also His messenger.'" He then said to me: "How should the *khutba* be read for me?" I replied: "In your name and the name of your father." He said, "My father was an unbeliever, and I do not like to mention his name on the pulpit. And I too do not like to have my name mentioned, because he who gave me the name was an unbeliever. But what is the name of my master, the Commander of the Faithful?" I said: "Ja'far." He said: "Is it possible for me to be called by this name?" "Yes," I replied. He said: "Then I have decided that my name is to be Ja'far, and that of my father 'Abdallah. Please instruct the scribe accordingly." And I did so.

From then on the *khutba* was read for him: "O God, prosper your servant Ja'far ibn 'Abdallah, Amir of the Bulghars, the client of the Commander of the Faithful."

When three days had passed after the reading of the letter and delivery of the gifts, he sent for me, having come to know of the four thousand dinars, and how the ruse of the Christian had resulted in delaying the payment thereof. Information concerning this matter was contained in the letter.

When I entered his presence, he bade me be seated, and I sat down. He threw the letter of the Commander of the Faithful to me and said: "Who brought this letter?" I replied: "I did." He then said: "And the money that has been mentioned in both of them, what has been done with it?" I said: "It was impossible to collect it. Time was short, and we feared lest we fail to gain entry [into the land of the Turks on time]. We left the money behind to catch up with us later." He said: "You came, the whole lot of you, and my master spent what he spent on you, only in order that his money be brought to me, so that I might build a fortress which would protect me from the Jews who have enslaved me. As for the gifts, my slave would have been able to bring them." I said: "It is as you say! However, we did our best." He told the interpreter: "Tell him: 'I do not know these others; I only know you, for these are a non-Arab people. Had the Caliph, may God support him, thought they were capable of doing what you could do, he would not have sent you to safeguard my interests, to read [his letter] to me, and to listen to my response. I will not demand a single *dirham* from anyone but you. Give up the money. It is better for you."

I left his presence frightened and distressed. He was a man of striking appearance and dignity, stout and broad, who sounded as though he were speaking from inside a large barrel. I left him, gathered my colleagues and acquainted them with what had passed between him and me. I said to them: "This is what I had been afraid of."

His *mu'adhin* [caller to prayer] used to double the *iqama* [exhortation] when he performed the call to prayer. So I said to the king: "Your master, the Commander of the Faithful, recites the formulas of the exhortation only once in his abode." He told the caller: "Accept what he tells you and do not contradict him."

The caller kept this up for a few days as the king continued to question me about the money, and to debate the matter with me, while I did not cease to argue and to make him despair of it. When he had lost all hope of getting it he ordered the caller to double [the formulas of] the exhortation, and he did so. He intended by this to create an issue as a means for debating the matter with me. When I heard the caller doubling the exhortation, I forbade him to do so, and shouted at him. The king heard of this, and caused me and my companions to be brought into his presence.

When we had assembled he said to the interpreter: "Tell him (meaning me), what does he say concerning two callers, one of

Wall painting of Bactrian ambassador to Afrasiyab, Samarkand, 7th cent.

whom recites the formulas of the exhortation once, and the other recites them twice, then each of them leads a group of people in the ritual prayer. Is the prayer valid or invalid?" I said; "The prayer is valid." He said: "In accordance with differences of legal opinion, or in accordance with consensus?" I said; "In accordance with consensus." "Tell him, what does he say about a man who entrusted certain men with money intended for a group of weak, blockaded and enslaved people, and they betrayed him?" I said: "That is not permitted, and these are evil people." He said; "According to different legal opinions, or according to consensus?" I said: "According to consensus."

He said to the interpreter: "Tell him, were the Caliph, may God prolong his life, to send an army against me, would it prevail over me?" I said: "No." He said: "And the *amir* of Khurasan?" I said: "No." He said: "Is that not because of the remoteness of the distance and the multitude of tribes of unbelievers which lie between us?" I said: "Yes." He said: "Tell him: 'I swear by God, although I happen to be in my distant abode wherein you see me, yet I am afraid of my master the Commander of the Faithful. That is because he might come to hear something about me he might not like, and that, as a consequence, he might pray to God and cause me to perish in my own abode, while he is in his kingdom, and between him and me lie vast distances. Yet you who eat his bread and wear his clothes, and see him at all times, have betrayed him with regard to the mission on which he sent you to me, to a weak people, and you have betrayed the Muslims! I will not accept [guidance] from you in a matter pertaining to my religion until there comes to me a man who cherishes my welfare in what he says. When a man of this type comes to me, I will be receptive to him.'" We were rendered speechless and were unable to answer him, and thus we departed from his presence.

After this statement he began to favor me [over others] and to draw me close to his person, while keeping my companions at a distance. He began calling me Abu Bakr as-Siddiq.

I saw in his country marvels, which I am unable to enumerate because of their great number. Among them was the strangest: the first night we spent in his country, an hour before sunset, I saw the horizon turn intensely red, and I heard powerful noises and a loud hum coming from the atmosphere. I beheld a red, fire-like cloud close to me, and the hum and the noises seemed to be coming from it. Within it there seemed to be something similar to men and horses, and in the hands of these phantoms resembling men there were spears and swords which I could both clearly make out and envision myself. In the meantime there appeared another cloud, which was similar to the first, wherein I could see men, horses and weapons. This mass then began to attack the other in the same manner that one cavalry detachment attacks another. We were frightened by this phenomenon and turned to supplication and prayer, while the people [of the town] laughed at us and expressed their astonishment at our actions.

We watched one detachment attack another, the two mingling for a while and then separating. The phenomenon continued in this fashion for a part of the night, then the two groups disappeared. We asked the king about this [matter], and he alleged that his forefathers used to say that these were the believers and the unbelievers among the *jinn*, who battled each other every evening, and that they have not done without this battle for a single night for as long as they have existed.

A tailor in the service of the king, from among the residents of Baghdad, had happened to come to that region, and entered my tent with the object of conversing. We talked for the amount of time it takes for a man to read less than one half of one seventh of the Quran. While awaiting the call for the evening prayer, suddenly we heard the call for prayer. We went out of the tent and dawn had broken already. I said to the caller: "Which call for prayer did you make?" He said: "The call for the dawn prayer." I said: "And the evening prayer?" He said: "We perform it together with the sunset prayer." I said: "And the

Bulghar horseman with captive, depicted on golden vessel
from the treasure of Nagyszentmiklós

night?" He said: "It is as you see. It used to be shorter than this, but has now started to grow longer." He mentioned that he had not slept since before a month lest the morning prayer elude him. That is because a man can put a pot on the fire at the time of the sunset prayer, and then perform the evening prayer without its having had time to boil.

I saw that their day is extremely long for a certain time of the year, while the night is short. Then the night is long and the day short. On the second night I sat outside my tent and watched the sky. I did not see more than a small number of stars, which I estimated to be about fifteen stars, scattered about. It was clear that the red glow that precedes the sunset never disappears, and that the night is not too dark, so that a man can recognize another from a distance greater than a bow shot.

I saw that the moon does not occupy the center of the sky [in these regions], but rises for a while in the outer parts thereof; the dawn then breaks and the moon sets. The king told me that at a distance of three months journey beyond his country, there is a people called Wisu, in whose land the duration of the night is less than an hour.

I saw the country at sunrise, wherein everything turns red, the earth, the mountains, and all that a man looks at when the sun rises, resembling as it does a great cloud. The redness continues in the manner described until the sun reaches the highest point in the sky. I was informed by the residents of the country that when it is wintertime, the night attains to the length of day, and the day attains to the shortness of the night. The phenomenon is such that when one of us goes forth to a place called Itil, between which place and us there is less than the distance of a *farsakh*'s journey, at daybreak, he does not reach it until dark, until the time when all the stars have risen and covered the sky. We did not leave the country until the night had become long and the day short.

I saw that the inhabitants of this country regard the barking of dogs as very auspicious, and they rejoice at it, saying: "It will be a year of fertility, blessings, and well being." I found snakes to be abundant in their land to the extent that a branch of a tree will have ten or more snakes entwined around it. The natives do not kill the snakes and the snakes do not harm them. I once saw in a certain locality a tall tree, which was more than a hundred cubits long. This tree, which had fallen down, had a trunk of great magnitude. I stopped to look at it, when it began to move, a fact that frightened me. As I looked at it closely, I saw on the trunk a snake that was close to it in thickness and length. When it saw me, the snake dropped from it and disappeared among the trees. I was terrified and came and told the king and those in his company, but they did not show any interest in the matter. And the king said: "Do not be distressed; they will not harm you."

We alighted with the king at a camp site, and my companions, Tekin, Sausan, Bars, and I, together with a man from among the companions of the king, went in among the trees and came upon a small green stalk, thin like a spindle but longer, from which grew a green shoot. On top of the shoot broad leaves stretched out on the ground, and were spread over it like a freshly sprouted plant. On it were berries, which no one who ate them would doubt that they were sweet pomegranates. Consequently we did not cease to seek them out and eat them.

I saw that they have apples of a very vivid green color, and more sour than wine vinegar. Young girls eat them, and they are called "girl apples." I saw nothing more abundant in their country than hazelnut trees. I saw [a number of] forests of these trees, of which [the extent of] one forest was forty *farsakhs* by a similar number of *farsakhs* in width.

I saw certain trees they have, the nature of which I do not know. They were extremely tall trees, the trunks of which were bare of leaves. The tops of those trees were similar to the tops of palm trees in that they had [fine] fronds, except that they were more closely set together. The natives single out a spot on the trunk, which they [seem to] know, where they drill a hole, beneath which they place a vessel. There flows into the vessel a liquid that is more delicious than honey. If a man drinks very much of it, it makes him drunk in the same manner as wine.

Most of what they eat is millet and horsemeat, although wheat and barley are plentiful. Everyone who grows something takes it for himself, the king having no claim to it. However, they render to him every year a sable skin from each household. When the king orders a raiding party to make a foray against a country, and booty is taken, he along with them is due a share. It is incumbent on anyone who holds a wedding feast, or invites a guest to a banquet, that the king receives a portion commensurate with the size of the feast, as well as a bowl of honey drink, and some bad wheat. It is bad because their soil is black and putrid. They have no places for the storage of their food. Consequently, they dig wells in the ground and put the food in them. After a few days it begins to turn, becomes malodorous, and cannot be made use of.

They have neither olive oil, nor sesame oil, nor cooking oil of any kind. They use instead of these oils fish oil, and everything that they use reeks of fish oil. They make a soup from barley, which they feed to both the female and male slaves. Sometimes they cook the barley with meat. The masters eat the meat while the barley is fed to the slave girls, unless it be the head of a goat, in which case the slave girls are fed meat.

All of them wear caps. When the king rides forth, he rides alone without a servant, nor is there anyone else with him. When he passes through the market, there is no one who does not stand up, take his cap off from his head and put it under his arm. When he has gone past them, they return their caps to their heads. In like manner, all those who go before the king, both young and old, even his own children and his brothers, as soon as they look upon the king, they take off their caps and put them under their arms. They then make a gesture to him with their heads and sit down, and then they stand up again until he bids them be seated. Whoever sits in the presence of the king sits in

Turkic tribespeople with tents in Central Asia

a kneeling posture, and does not take out his cap, nor does he make it visible until he leaves the presence of the king, at which times he puts it on.

All of them live in tents, but the tent of the king is extremely large, holding up to a thousand persons and more. It is spread with Armenian carpets, and in the center of it the king has a throne covered with Greek brocade.

Among their customs is the fact that when a male child is born to the son of a certain man, his grandfather and not his father takes him, saying: "I have more right to raise him until he reaches the state of manhood than his own father." When a man dies among them, his brother rather than his son becomes his heir. I informed the king that this was unlawful, and explained [the principles of] inheritance [according to Muslim law] until he understood them.

I have never encountered more thunderbolts than in their country. When a thunderbolt falls on a house, they do not go near it, saying: "This house is the object of [divine] wrath."

When one of their men willfully kills another, they kill him in retaliation. If he kills him by mistake, they make a box for him out of birch wood, put him inside it, and nail him up in it. They put with him three flat loaves of bread and a jug of water. They set up for him three poles similar to the poles on a camel's saddle, and hang the box between them. They say: "We put him between heaven and earth so that the rain and sun get to him. It may be that God will have mercy on him." He remains hanging until time wears him out, and the winds scatter him abroad.

When they see a man who is possessed of a certain [mental] agility and knowledge of things, they say: "It is fitting for this man that he should serve our Lord." They then seize him, put a rope around his neck and hang him on a tree until he disintegrates.

The king's interpreter told me that a man from Sind happened to have come to that country and stayed for a time with the king in order to serve him. He was a lively and perceptive person. A group of them were about to embark upon a commercial undertaking [?], and the man from Sind asked the king for permission to accompany them. The king forbade him to do so, but the man persisted until the king gave his permission. He departed with them in a boat, and they saw that he was an adroit and nimble-minded person. They deliberated among themselves and decided: "This man is well suited to serve our Lord, so let us dispatch him to Him." While traveling they passed through a forest. They consequently brought him out there, put a rope around his neck, and tied him to the top of a tall tree, where they left him and went on their way.

If they happen to be traveling along a road, and one of them wants to urinate, and he does so while carrying his weapons, they plunder him, taking his weapons and his clothes, and all that he has with him. This is a custom of theirs. He, however, who lays down his weapons, placing them aside while he urinates, they do not molest him.

The men and the women go down to the river and bathe together naked, without covering themselves one from the other. They do not commit fornication in any manner whatsoever. He among them who commits fornication, whoever he may be, they set out four stakes in the ground for him, tie his hands and feet to them, and cleave him with an axe from the scruff of his neck to his thighs. They do the same to the [guilty] woman also. They then hang each piece of him and of her on a tree.

I did not cease to strive [to induce them] to make the women cover themselves from the men while swimming, but I did not succeed in my endeavors. They kill the thief as they kill the fornicator.

In their forests there is much honey [found] in the [wild] beehives known to them, and they go out in quest of it. Sometimes a group from among their enemies falls upon them and kills them. Among them are merchants who go out to the land of the Turks and bring back sheep, and to the country called Wisu and return with sable and black fox.

We saw among them members of a family known as Baranjar, comprising five thousand souls of both men and women, all of whom had embraced Islam. They had built for themselves a mosque of wood in which they performed the ritual prayer. They could not read [the Quran], and I taught a group of them that which was necessary to perform the prayer.

A man had accepted Islam at my hands whose name was Talut, and I named him 'Abdallah. He said: "I want you to call me by your name Muhammad." And I did. His wife, his mother, and his children accepted Islam and were all of them called Muhammad. I taught him: "Praise be to God," and "Say, He is God the One," and his joy at having come to know these two *suras* [verses of the Quran] was greater than his joy might have been had he become the king of the Saqaliba.

When we came to the king, we found them encamped by a water called Khallaja, which consists of three lakes, two large and one small, except that in none of them can the bottom be reached. Between this place and a large river of theirs which flows into the land of the Khazars, and which is called the river

Itil, is approximately one *farsakh*. On this river is the site of a
market, which takes place periodically, in which much precious
merchandise is sold.

Tekin had told me that in the land of the king was a man with
a gigantic physique. When we arrived in the country, I asked the
king about him. He said: "Yes. He used to be in our country and
died here. He was not of the people of this land, nor was he of
human kind. His story is as follows: Some people from among
the merchants went out to the river Itil, a river between which
and us there is a distance of one day, as they were wont to do.
This river had risen and its water had overflowed its banks.
Then one day, all of a sudden, a group of merchants came to me
saying: 'O king, there has come floating on the water a man,
who if he is from a people near to us, it is no longer possible for
us to stay in these regions, and [we] have no choice but to move
elsewhere.' I rode out with them until I reached the river, and
behold, there was the man who measured twelve cubits of those
in use in my realm. He had a head that was as large as the
largest cooking pot, a nose that measured more than a span, two
enormous eyes, and fingers each of which measured more than
a span. I was awed by him and was overcome by the same ter-
ror that had overcome the others. We started to speak to him,
but he did not speak to us and only gazed at us.

"I brought him to the place where I was staying and wrote to
the people of Wisu, who are three months distant from us, with
the purpose of asking them about him. They wrote informing
me that this man was from Gog and Magog, [a people] who are
three months distant from us. They are naked, and the sea forms
a barrier between them and us, for they are located on its shore.
They are like beasts that go about copulating with each other.
God, might and majesty be His, brings out for them every day a
fish from the sea. A man of them comes with a knife and cuts off
a quantity that is sufficient for him and his family. If, however,
he takes more than meets his needs, he complains of stom-
achache, as do members of his family who also complain of their

stomachs. Sometimes he, and indeed the whole lot of them, may die. When they take from the fish what they need, it turns over and falls back into the sea. They keep doing so every day.

"Between us and them on one side is the sea, and they are surrounded by mountains on the other sides. Also the wall lies as a barrier between them and the gate through which they were wont to pass. When God, might and majesty be His, wishes to turn them out on the habitable world, he will cause an opening in the wall and a drying up of the sea, and the fish will be cut off from them."

I then asked him about the man and he said; "He stayed with me for a time. No boy who looked at him could help but suffer death, and no pregnant woman could help suffering a miscarriage. If he happened to overcome a man, he squeezed him with his two hands until he killed him. When I saw this, I hung him upon a tall tree until he died. If you would like to look at his bones and his head, I will take you to see them." I said: "By God, I should like that." And he rode out with me to a large forest in which were huge trees. He went ahead of me to a tree under which the giant's bones and head had fallen, and I saw his head, which was like a large beehive, and his ribs, which were bigger than the base of date palm branches. So were also the bones of both his legs and his two forearms. I marveled at him and left.

The king moved from the water they call Khallaja to a river named Jaushir, and stayed there for two months. He then wanted to leave, and sent to a people called Suwaz, instructing them to depart with him. They refused and split into two factions. One faction was with his son-in-law, who had proclaimed himself king over them and whose name was Wirigh. The king sent [a message] to them saying: "God, might and majesty be His, has bestowed upon me the blessings of Islam and the power of the Commander of the Faithful. I am his servant, and this nation has invested me with authority [over its affairs]. Whoever opposes me, him shall I meet with the sword." The other faction was with a king of a tribe, who was known as King Eskel, and who owed allegiance to the king of the Saqaliba, although he had not joined [the community] of Islam.

When he sent his letter to them, they were awed by him, and all of them journeyed with him to the river Jaushir, which is a river of small width, its width being five cubits, and its water reaching to the navel, although there are places where it reaches the collarbone, while the greatest depth is a fathom. Around it are abundant trees consisting of birch trees and others.

Near this river is a vast wilderness wherein they say is an animal that is less than a camel and more like a bull in size. Its head is like the head of a camel, and its tail is like the tail of a bull, while its body is like the body of a mule, and its hooves are like the cloven hooves of a bull. In the center of its head, it has a thick round horn, which as it rises from the head of the animal gets to be thinner until it becomes like the point of a lance. The length of some of these horns is from three to five cubits, and there are those that may attain to a greater or lesser length. The animal grazes on the leaves of trees, which are quite green. When it sees a horseman, it makes straight for him, and if he happens to have under him a fast horse, he is rendered safe from it with some effort. If it overtakes him, it removes him from the back of his horse with its horn, hurls him into the air, and then catches him with its horn. It continues in this manner until it kills him. It does not bother the horse in any form or manner. They seek out this animal in the forests in order to kill it. They do that by climbing the tall trees among which it is found, and with this object in mind, they assemble a number of archers with poisoned arrows. When it stands in their midst, they shoot at it until it is severely wounded and killed by them.

I saw in the king's house three large bowls which looked like [they were made of] the onyx of Yemen. The king informed me that it was made from the base of the horn of the animal. Some of the people of the country told me that it was a rhinoceros.

I did not see among them a man with a ruddy complexion; rather most of them were ailing. It is often the case that most of them die from colic, so that it afflicts even the nursing infant among them. When a Muslim dies in their country, or when the husband of a woman from Khwarazm dies, they wash him in the manner of the Muslims. Then they place him on a cart, which carries him along, while a standard goes in front of him, until they take him to the place in which they are to bury him. When his body reaches the [burial] place, they remove him from the cart and place him on the ground. Then they draw a line around him, and set him aside. They then dig his grave within the aforementioned line, which they make his resting place wherein he is buried. That is what they do with their dead.

The women do not cry over the dead man, rather it is the men among them who weep over him. They come on the day in which he dies and stand at the door of his tent. They then give vent to the most disgusting and uncanny wailing. These are the freeborn men. When their crying is done, slaves arrive carrying braided strands of leather. They do not cease to cry and to beat their sides and the uncovered parts of their bodies with those thongs until there appears on their bodies something similar to welts caused by whip strokes. They inevitably raise a standard at the door of the dead man's tent. They bring his weapons and place them around his grave. They do not stop crying for two years. When the two years have passed, they haul down the standard and cut their hair. The relatives of the dead man issue an invitation to a meal, which is a sign indicating that they are coming out of mourning, and if he happens to have had a wife, she remarries. This is so if he happens to be one of their chiefs. As regards the common people, they perform only some of these rites for their dead.

There is imposed on the king of the Saqaliba a tribute that he pays to the king of the Khazars, namely a sable skin for each household in his kingdom. When a ship from the country of the Khazars arrives in the country of the Saqaliba, the king rides out, takes stock of what is on board, and takes a tenth of the entire merchandise. When the Rus, or the members of some other races, come with slaves, the king has the right to choose for himself one out of every ten head.

The son of the king of the Saqaliba is held as a hostage at the court of the king of the Khazars. The king of the Khazars had learned of the beauty of the daughter of the king of the Saqaliba, and sent [an emissary] asking for her hand in marriage. The king of the Saqaliba protested and refused his request. Whereupon the king of the Khazars sent troops and seized her by force, although he was a Jew and she was a Muslim, and she died at his court. He then sent an emissary asking for the hand of another of his daughters. As soon as the king of the Saqaliba learned of this, he acted without delay and married her off to the king of the Eskel, who was subject to him, out of fear that the king of the Khazars might seize her by force, as he had done with her sister. What induced the king of the Saqaliba to write and ask the Caliph to build a fortress for him was his fear of the king of the Khazars.

I asked him one day saying to him: "Your kingdom is extensive, your wealth abundant, and your tax revenues are many. Why did you ask the Caliph to build a fortress with an amount of money from his coffers that is of no account?" He said: "I found the empire of Islam to be prosperous, and recourse may be had to its lawfully derived revenues. I sought these funds for this reason. Had I wanted to build a fortress of silver or gold with my own money, the attainment of such an object would not have been difficult for me. I merely sought to benefit from the blessing that attaches to the money of the Commander of the Faithful, and for which reason I asked him for it."

The Rus

I saw the Rusiya when they came hither on their trading voyages and had encamped by the river Itil. I have never seen people with a more developed bodily stature than they. They are as tall as date palms, blond and ruddy, so that they do not need to wear a tunic nor a cloak; rather the men among them wear a garment that only covers half of his body and leaves one of his hands free.

Each of them has an axe, a sword, and a knife with him, and all of these whom we have mentioned never let themselves be separated from their weapons. Their swords are broad bladed, provided with rills, and of the Frankish type. Each one of them has from the tip of his nails to the neck figures, trees, and other things, tattooed in dark green.

Each of the women has fastened upon the two breasts a brooch of iron, silver, copper, or gold, in weight and value according to the wealth of her husband. Each brooch has a ring to which a knife is likewise fixed, and is hung upon the breast. Around the neck the women wear rings of gold and silver.

The man, if he possesses ten thousand *dirhams*, has a neck ring made for his wife. If he has twenty thousand in his possession, then he has two neck rings made for her. And so his wife receives another neck ring with the addition of each ten thousand *dirhams*. Accordingly it often happens that there are a number of neck rings upon the neck of one of them. They consider as the most highly prized ornaments the green glass beads made out of clay, which are formed on the polishing stone. They bargain for these beads, and buy a bead for a *dirham* a piece, and string them into necklaces for their women.

They are the dirtiest creatures of God. They have no shame in voiding their bowels and bladder, nor do they wash themselves when polluted by emission of semen, nor do they wash their hands after eating. They are then like asses who have gone astray.

Portage on Russian rivers as depicted by Olaus Magnus

They come from their own country, moor their boats on the strand of the Itil, which is a great river, and build on its banks large houses out of wood. In a house like this ten or twenty people, more or less, live together. Each of them has a couch whereupon he sits, and with them are fair maidens who are destined for sale to the merchants, and they may have intercourse with their girl while their comrades look on. At times a crowd of them may come together, and one does this in the presence of the others. It also happens that a merchant, who comes into the house to buy a girl from one of them, may find him in the very act of having intercourse with her, and he [the Rus] will not let her be until he has fulfilled his intention.

As a matter of duty they wash daily their faces and heads in a manner so dirty, and so unclean, as could possibly be imagined. Thus it is carried out. A slave girl brings each morning early a large vessel with water, and gives the vessel to her master, and he washes his hands and face and the hair of his head. He washes it and combs it with a comb into the bucket, then blows his nose and spits into the bucket. He holds back nothing impure, but rather lets it go into the water.

After he has done what was necessary, the girl takes the same vessel to the one who is nearest, and he does just as his neighbor had done. She carries the vessel from one to another, until all in the house have had a turn at it, and each of them has blown his nose, spat into, and washed his face and hair in the vessel.

When their boats come to this anchorage, each one of them goes ashore with bread, meat, onions, milk, and mead, and betakes himself to a tall wooden pole set upright, that has a face like a man. Around it are small images and behind these are long, tall poles driven into the earth. And he comes to the great image and prostrates himself before it. Then he says: "O my lord, I have come from a far country and have with me so many slave girls for such a price, and so many sable pelts," until he has enumerated all the goods which he has brought for sale. Then he continues: "I have brought this offering to Thee." Then he lays down what he had brought before the wooden image and continues: "I wish that Thou shouldst provide me with a merchant who has many *dinars* and *dirhams*, and who would buy from me at the price I desire, and will raise no objection to me to aught what I may say." Then he departs.

If he has difficulties in his trading, and the days of his stay are prolonged, then he makes a second and a third offering. Should difficulties again arise over what he hopes to attain, he then brings a gift to each of these little figures, and begs them to intercede, saying: "These are the wives, daughters, and sons of our lord." And so he continues to approach each image, one after the other, and to beg them and implore them to intercede, and prays before them in abasement.

His dealings often go on more easily, and he sells everything he has brought with them. Then he says: "My lord has fulfilled my desire. I must repay Him." He gathers a number of sheep and oxen, slaughters them, gives away a part of the meat as alms, and brings the remainder and casts it before that great wooden image and before the little wooden images which stand around it. He hangs the heads of the cattle, or those of the sheep, on the poles, which are erected in the earth. In the night the dogs come and devour all, and he who has made this sacrifice says: "Verily my lord is content with me, and he has eaten up my gift."

If one of them falls ill, they erect a tent for him at a distance from themselves, and leave him there. They put beside him a little bread and water, do not approach him, and do not speak to him. Indeed what is still more, they do not visit him at all during all the days of his illness, especially if he is weak or if he is a slave. When he has recovered and gets up, he comes back to them. If, however, he dies, they cremate him. If he is a slave they let him be, and then the dogs and carrion fowl devour him.

If they catch a thief or a robber, they lead him to a thick tree, throw a trusty rope around his neck and hang him to the tree, and he remains hanging until with the wind and the rain he falls to pieces.

They told me that they carry out many ceremonies when their chiefs die, the least whereof is the cremation, and it interested me to find out more about it. Finally the news was brought to me that a prominent man among them had died. They laid him in a grave, and covered it with a roof for ten days until they were through with the cutting out and sewing together of his garments. Thus it is; if [the dead] is poor they make a boat and place him in it and burn the boat. If he is a rich man, they gather his possessions together and divide them in three parts. One third remains for his family; with the second third they cut out garments for him, and with third part they brew mead for themselves, which they drink on the day when his slave girl kills herself and is cremated with her master. They drink the mead to insensibility, day and night. It often happens that one of them dies with his beaker in his hand.

When a high chief dies, his family says to his slave girls and servants: "Which one of you wishes to die with him?" Then one of them answers: "I." When he [or she] has said this he is bound. He can in no way be allowed to withdraw his word. If he wishes it, it is not permitted. For the most part, this self-sacrifice is made by the maidens.

When the above-mentioned man had died, his relatives said to his slave girls: "Who will die with him?" Thereupon one of them answered: "I." Then the relations of the deceased charged two girls to watch her and go with her wherever she went. Indeed they even washed her feet with their own hands. The relatives of the deceased then began to occupy themselves with the preparations for the funeral ceremonies, to have the garments cut out for him, and to prepare whatever was necessary. The slave girl meanwhile drank all day long and sang joyfully, and enjoyed herself in view of the future.

When the day had come on which he and the maiden should be cremated, I put in an appearance at the river where his bark lay. I saw that this already had been hauled up on land. There were four props set up for the boat, of birch and other wood, and around the boat had been built a large structure like a large scaffold of wood. Then they hauled the ship further up, until it was placed inside this structure.

The people then began to move hither and thither, and to speak words that I did not understand, while he was still lying in his grave, out of which they had not taken him. Then they brought a couch, placed it on the ship, and covered it with draperies of Byzantine brocade, and also with pillows of Byzantine brocade.

Thereupon an old woman came, whom they call the angel of death, and spread the draperies mentioned over the couch. She had held the oversight over the sewing of the garments of the deceased and their completion. This old woman kills the girl. I saw that she was an old giantess, fat and grim to behold.

When they came to his grave, they removed the earth from the timbers and raised the timbers, drew him forth in the same garment in which he had died, and I saw how he had turned black from the cold earth. I also noted that they had put in his grave mead, fruits, and a kind of mandolin. They now took all of these out of the grave. Naught had changed in the deceased apart from the color of his skin. They then dressed him in stockings, trousers, boots, [and] a tunic and cape of brocade with gold buttons. They put a cap of brocade and sable pelts upon him and carried him into the tent that had been erected on the boat. Here they placed him upon the quilts, propped him up with cushions, brought mead, fruits, and flowers, and laid these beside him. They also brought bread, meat, and onions, and strewed them before him. Then they brought a dog, cleft it in two halves, and laid it in the boat. Thereupon they brought all his weapons and laid them by his side. Then they took two horses, drove them until they perspired, then cleft both of them in twain with a sword and laid their flesh in the boat. Then they brought two cows, cut them in two likewise and laid them in the boat. Then they brought a cock and a hen, killed them and threw both into the ship. The maiden who wished to be put to death went here and there, and entered each of the tents where the head of each tent had intercourse with her saying: "Say to thy lord, I have done this out of love of thee."

On Friday in the afternoon they brought the maiden to a structure, which they had erected like a doorframe. She put both her feet on the palms of the men, and was lifted up onto this doorframe, and said her piece. Then they let her down again. Thereupon they put her up a second time. She repeated what she had done the first time, and then they let her down, and let her go up a third time. Again she did as she had done on the first two occasions. Then they gave her a hen. She cut off its head and cast it away. They took the hen and laid it in the boat. Thereupon I asked the interpreter what her actions meant. He said: "When they raised her up the first time, she said: 'Behold, I see my father and mother'; the second time she said: 'There I see all my deceased relatives sitting'; the third time she said: 'There I behold my lord sitting in paradise, and paradise is fair and green, and around him are men and servants. He calls me; bring me to him.'"

Then they led her to the boat. She took off the two armlets that she wore and gave them to the old woman whom they call the angel of death, who was to kill her. Then the slave girl took off two anklets that she had and gave them to the two maidens who had waited on her, and who were the daughters of the old woman known as the angel of death.

Then the people lifted her onto the boat, but did not yet let her go into the tent. Hereupon came men with shields and staves and gave her a bowl of mead, whereupon she sang and drank it. The interpreter said to me: "With this she is bidding goodbye to her friends." Then she was given another beaker. She took it and sang for a long time, while the old woman was urging her to finish the goblet, and to go into the tent where her lord lay.

I saw then how disturbed she was. She wished to go into the tent, but put her head between the tent and the side of the boat. Then the old woman took her by the head, made her go into the tent, and also entered with her.

Whereupon the men began to beat their shields with the staves so that her shrieks would not be heard, and the other maidens become terrified. Then six men went into the tent, and all had intercourse with the girl. Then they placed her beside her dead lord; two men seized her by the feet and two by the hands. Then the old woman placed a rope in which a bight had been made, and gave it to two of the men to pull at the two ends.

Then the old woman came to her with a broad-bladed dagger and began to jab it into her ribs and pull it out again, and the two men strangled her until she was dead.

After they had laid the maiden they had killed beside her master, wood for kindling the fire was prepared. The closest relative of the deceased approached, and took a piece of wood, kindled it and then walked backwards to the boat, keeping his face turned toward the spectators, holding the burning brand in one hand, and placing his other on his anus. He was naked and walked backwards until he reached the boat and set fire to the wood that had been prepared beneath the boat. Then the people came with kindling and other firewood, each having a brand burning at the end, and laid this stick in the pile of wood. Fire then spread through the wood and spread to the kindling, the boat, the man, the maiden, and everything that was in the boat. A strong and violent wind sprang up through which the flames were fanned and greatly enhanced.

A man of the Rusiya was standing beside me and I heard him talking to the interpreter, and I asked what the Rus had said to him. The interpreter answered that he said: "They, the Arab communities, are stupid." So I asked: "Why?" He said: "You go and cast into the earth the people whom you both love and honor most among men. Then the earth, creeping things, and worms devour them. We, however, let them burn for an instant, and accordingly he enters into paradise at once in that very hour," and he burst into immoderate laughter.

He said: "His Lord sent the wind for love of him, so that he may be snatched away in the course of an hour." In fact an hour had not passed when boat, wood, maiden, and lord had turned to ashes and dust of ashes. Then they built on the site of the boat that they had hauled up out of the stream something like a rounded mound. In the middle of this they erected a great beam of birch wood, and wrote upon it the name of the man and the name of the king of the Rus, whereupon they departed.

One of the customs of the king of the Rusiya is that with him in his palace he has four hundred men from among his most valiant and trusted men. They die when he dies and are killed for his sake. Each one has a slave girl who waits on him, washes his head, and prepares for him what he eats and drinks. He has another slave girl with whom he has intercourse. These four hundred sit under his throne, which is a large throne, studded with precious gems. Forty slave girls, who are intended for his bed, sit by him on his throne. He may have sexual intercourse with one of them in the presence of the companions whom we have mentioned. He does not come down from the throne. Whenever he wants to answer a call to nature, he does it in a basin. When he wishes to ride they bring him his horse to the throne, and he mounts it from the throne. When he wishes to dismount he brings the horse so that he dismounts from it onto the throne. He has a viceroy who leads his armies, attacks the foe, and represents him before his people.

The Khazars
(from Yaqut, including a section of Ibn Fadlan)

Khazar is the name of a region whose chief city is called Itil. Itil is also the name of a river that flows to Khazar from the Rus and Bulghars. Itil is a city while Khazar is the name of a kingdom and not the name of a city. There are two parts to Itil; on the west side of the river it is called Itil, which is the larger part. On the east side lives the king, who in their language is called Ilek, and he is also called Bak [Beg]. The western part in size is about a *farsakh* in length and around it is a wall. There are no buildings, for their houses are tents of felt, except a few structures built of clay; they do have bazaars and baths. In the town are many Muslims. It is said that there are more than ten thousand and they have about thirty mosques.

The palace of the king is far from the banks of the river, and his palace is built of brick, and it is the only structure built of bricks, and the only one permitted to be built of brick. The [city] wall has four gates, one of which opens to the river, while the others lead to the plain on the backside of the city.

Their king is Jewish, and it is said he has about four thousand courtiers. In Khazar [land] are Christians, Muslims, and idol worshippers, but the fewest are the Jews, and the king is among them. Most are Muslims and Christians, while the king and his followers are Jews. The major part of their customs, however, are those of the idol worshippers, some of whom prostrate themselves to others in their homage. The laws of their domain are different rules than those of the Muslims, Jews, and Christians. The roster of the army of the king is twenty thousand men, and when one of them dies another is made to take his place, and the number is never less than that amount. They do not have official rations except a sparse amount that is given to them for a long period when they are at war, or if a catastrophe befalls them, for which they assemble. The principal revenue of the Khazars is from tolls and tithes on trading according to their rules, [on traders coming] from every way, sea, and river. And they have support payments to the local people and surrounding [places] of all kinds, whatever they have need of—food, drink, and the like.

And the king has nine judges of Jews, Christians, Muslims, and idol worshippers. If a legal case arises for some people these [judges] adjudicate it. Those in need do not contact the king himself, [but] rather those judges contact him. Between the king and those judges there is, on the day of judging, an emissary [go-between] whom they send concerning what has transpired to apprise [the king of it], and he would return his orders to them, and they would conclude it.

This city has no suburbs, except broad fields; they go out in the summer to the fields, about twenty *farsakhs*. Then they till and harvest them. When some of the [fields] adjoin the river they transport [the harvest] by boats, and from other fields by carts to the river. Most of their food is rice and fish, and whatever else is found among them is brought to them from Rus and Bulghar and Kiev. And in the eastern part of the city of the Khazars are most of the merchants, Muslims, and warehouses [?].

The language of the Khazars is different from that of the Turks and of Persians, and it is unlike any other human tongue. The Khazars do not resemble the Turks, and they have black hair, and there is a group of them who are called Qara [black] Khazars, ranging from very tawny to black, as if they were a group from India. There is another group, white, handsome and beautiful in appearance, and they consist of the slaves of the Khazars. They are the people of idols who permit enslaving and selling their children to others, but for Jews and Christians, according to their religions, such sale is forbidden, similar to Muslims. Nothing is exported from the land of the Khazars to another land except what they import, such as flour, honey, wax, silk, and furs.

Ibn Fadlan says: The king of the Khazars is called Khaqan, and he only appears in public promenading once every four months. He is called the great Khaqan and his viceroy is called Khaqan Bih. It is the latter that leads and controls the armed forces, conducts affairs of the kingdom, appears before the people, and leads raids [on enemies]. It is to him that the neighboring kings submit. Every day he humbly goes to the great Khaqan, showing humility and deference. He does not go into his presence except barefoot and carrying firewood in his arms. When he greets him [the ruler] he kindles the fire in front of him, and when he has finished lighting the fire with the firewood, he sits with the king at his right side on the throne. The Khaqan Bih is represented by [another] man who is called Kundur Khaqan, and that one is represented by a man who is called Jaushighir. A custom of the king is that he does not sit and receive people in audience, nor does he speak to them, nor does anyone other

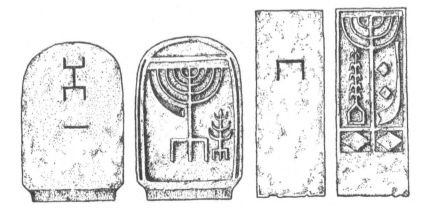

Khazar Jewish gravestones from Phanagoreia

than those mentioned enter his presence. Powers of appointments and dismissals, and of imposing punishments, as well as management of the affairs of state, all are the responsibility of the Khaqan Bih.

It is a custom that when the great king dies a large house is built for him, in which are twenty excavated rooms, in each of which a sepulcher is dug. And stone is carved such that it is shaped like the firmament, and placed in the [house], and stones are crushed until they become like powder and spread on it [the floor?]. Below the building is a large river flowing, and they channel the river over that tomb so, as they say, that the devil cannot reach it, nor any person, nor any worms or serpents. When he is buried the company that buried him are beheaded, so it is not known where his grave is in those rooms. They call his grave heaven, and they say, verily he has entered heaven. And each of the rooms is covered with brocade with gold weave.

A custom of the king of the Khazars is that he has twenty-five wives, each of whom is a daughter of a neighboring king. He takes her voluntarily or by force. He has sixty concubines for his bed, each of whom is of surpassing beauty. Every one of them, free women and concubines, is placed in a separate palace; each has a cupola [?] covered with teak, and each surrounded by a large pavilion. Each woman has a eunuch who keeps her in seclusion. When the king wishes to have sexual intercourse with one of them, he sends to the eunuch who watches over her, and the eunuch brings her in the twinkling of an eye, and places her in his bed. The eunuch places himself at the door of the king's tent, and as soon as the king is through having intercourse with her, he takes her by the hand and leaves. Afterwards the eunuch does not leave her even for a minute.

When the king mounts his horse, all of his army follows his example, and there is a mile between him and the column. No one of his subjects sees him except falling on his face and prostrating before him, nor does one raise his head until he passes.

The period of rule of their king is forty years. When he exceeds it by one day, his subjects and followers kill him, saying: "This man's reason has failed, and his mind has become confused."

When he dispatches an army group, they do not turn their backs for any reason. If they are defeated, every one of them who returns is put to death. When his leaders and viceroy are put to flight, he brings them before him with their wives and children, and gives the latter as gifts to others in their presence while they are viewing it. He does the same with their horses, goods, weapons, and houses. Sometimes he cuts each of them in two pieces and exposes him on a gibbet. Sometimes he hangs them by their necks from trees, or if he is well disposed toward them he makes them stable servants.

The king of the Khazars has a large city on the river Itil, which is situated on both sides [of the river]. On one side are Muslims, while the king and his companions are on the other. Over the Muslims is a servant of the king called Khaz [khan?], who is himself a Muslim. Legal decisions concerning Muslims living in the land of the Khazars, and the Muslims who visit them in their trading activities, are referred to this Muslim servant. He alone looks into their affairs, and no one else acts as a judge among them.

The Muslims in this city have a Friday mosque in which they perform the prayers, and in which they gather on Fridays. It has a tall minaret and a number of callers [to prayer]. When news came to the king of the Khazars in 310 [922] that Muslims had destroyed the synagogue in Dar al-Babunaj, he ordered the minaret destroyed and killed the callers, saying: "If I had not feared that not one synagogue would remain in the realm of Islam, I would have destroyed the mosque."

The Khazars and their king are all Jews. The Saqaliba, and all those neighboring them, give obedience to the king. He speaks to them as to slaves, and they show him fealty. Some believe that Gog and Magog are the Khazars.

CHAPTER IV

Bulghar soldiers depicted in the Anglo-Saxon chronicle

Commentary on the Translation

Variant readings of the text of either the Meshhed manuscript or Yaqut, as well as philological notes, may be found in the items listed under translations in the bibliography. Both Togan and Kovalevskii give copious notes on variant readings in the text. Now that we know that the Meshhed manuscript is not the writing of Ibn Fadlan but a later compilation of geographical texts primarily concerned with inner Asia, one may guess that this compilation was made for a Turkic ruler, perhaps a Qarakhanid who ruled in Central Asia a century after our author. Certainly the manuscript is old, but further information about it is lacking. Let us turn to the text itself.

A number of general questions may be asked about the voyage of Ibn Fadlan. First, how did he travel? From Baghdad to Khwarazm, i.e. inside the domain of Islam or the *de jure* realm of the 'Abbasid Caliphate, he and his companions traveled along the Khurasan road (recently called the Silk Road), where stations for the postal service provided quarters for government couriers or officials. But it seems that he and his companions joined various caravans along stages of the voyage to Khwarazm. Beyond Khwarazm, however, he joined one caravan of merchants bound for the north. The caravan was large, according to our author: 5,000 men and 3,000 pack animals (probably mainly camels), which seems questionable but not impossible, since the number of riding horses or donkeys is not mentioned and many of the humans probably walked. At least one horse is mentioned—a present for the king of the Bulghars—but probably there were other riding, as well as pack, animals. In any case, it indicates the large size of the caravan, as well as the importance of the colony of Khwarazmians in the land of the Bulghars. They brought Islam, as well as objects of trade, to the north. Their influence is indicated by the old Russian word for Muslim or Musulman, which in the Russian texts, such as the *Russian Primary Chronicle* (also known as *Tales of Past Years*), is Busurman, a Khwarazmian pronunciation of the word.

Since there probably was a Sogdian merchant colony in the Crimea, and we know about Sogdian contacts with Byzantium, it would not be amiss to suggest that Sogdians joined the Khwarazmians in the trade to the north by the time of the Arab conquest in the seventh century. Even more speculative, but conceivable, is a proposal that there may have been an agreement between the Khwarazmian and Sogdian merchants that the former would concentrate on the northern trade routes, while the Sogdians controlled the routes to the Byzantine Empire. We do not know their relations with the Khazars, but inasmuch as trade was valued and even vital for all of the peoples of the north, merchants in general enjoyed a high status wherever they went. Rich caravans, however, always were open to attack and pillage not only by bandits but also by nomads. As a result, caravans were large, composed of many merchants joined together for protection and sharing the costs of hiring an armed escort. Only high profits from trade would tempt merchants to risk their lives and property on long voyages.

Our embassy, of course, was concerned with political and religious matters rather than trade, but commercial ties with the north could not be ignored. The ambassador of the group that made the expedition was Sausan al-Rasi, who was the client of Nadhir al-Hurami, vizier of the sultan. The use of the word "sultan" in the text of Ibn Fadlan is interesting, for it may imply a secular basis for the expedition: the government or state of the 'Abbasids, rather than simply the Caliph, who more and more was becoming only a religious figure, soon to be have his world-ly authority usurped by a secular ruler called the sultan.

If the ambassador is to be identified with a certain Sausan al-Jassasi, a eunuch in the court, as both Togan (1939, 3) and Kovalevskii (1956, 164) do, he was an important personage at the Caliphal court. Nadhir, also a eunuch according to several historical sources, may have been in charge of affairs or protocol at the Caliphal court, and if so he would not have accompanied the expedition. At the court in Baghdad, eunuchs were influential, since they had access to the Caliph and his harem. Some ambiguity is found in the text since Nadhir is called *safir*, which usually means ambassador, while Sausan is called *rasul*, which usually means messenger. Perhaps Nadhir had the role of ambassador—responsible for dealing with foreigners, including the Bulghars—whereas Sausan was merely the bearer of his written message. In any case, it is clear that Ibn Fadlan was responsible for the religious affairs of the embassy.

Another question is, with whom did he travel? Sausan al-Rasi, client of Nadhir al-Hurami, was part of the group, and he probably was entrusted with the medicine that the king of the Bulghars had requested from Nadhir, as well as with carrying letters from Nadhir. Further, we find 'Abdallah ibn Bashtu al-Khazari, a Muslim Khazar in the service of the king of the Bulghars as his envoy; Bars al-Saqlabi, probably the Bulghar translator; and Tekin al-Turki, the guide through the land of the Turks. These were the names of Ibn Fadlan's companions throughout his trip. Our author tells us that teachers, several specialists in Islamic law of law, and several pages who were to accompany the embassy to the Bulghars, after going with Ibn Fadlan as far as Khwarazm, decided to return to Baghdad in fear of the perils of the trip through the deserts into the land of the Turks. The use of plural for these persons at the beginning of the trip, but the singular when they left the embassy in Khwarazm, is puzzling. Either it is a lapse on the part of Ibn Fadlan, or by the time our group reached the land of the Turks, others had departed along the way.

The fact that the revenues from the estate of Ibn al-Furat, which were allocated for the salaries of the specialists in Islamic law and the teachers, had not been obtained from al-Fadl ibn Musa probably was just as important a reason for their leaving the embassy as fear of the unknown. After all, they must have realized from the beginning that the embassy was a dangerous undertaking. So Ibn Fadlan himself had to shoulder the burden of instruction in Islamic law and practices requested by the king of the Bulghars.

The itinerary through the realm of the Caliphate

If we follow his trip through Islamic regions to the land of the Turks, lengthy stops were made along the route, either waiting for another caravan going in the same direction or allowing the camels to rest. From Baghdad to Hulwan, at the foot of the Iranian plateau, the route followed was the time-honored direct road to the east, through Daskara, formerly called Dastgird, where the Sasanian kings had a palace. Qirmisin is present Kermanshah, the center of an area rich in agriculture and lower in elevation than Hamadan, ancient Ekbatana of the Medes. From Hamadan the land descended through Saveh to Ray, the ruins of which lie just south of Tehran. In Ray apparently they waited for an invitation to stay with the brother of the ruler of Ray, one Ahmad ibn 'Ali, who was in the district of Ray, so they moved at a leisurely pace to his quarters. He was the brother of Sa'luk, the ruler, a partisan of the Zaidis. The Zaidis were a moderate group of Shi'ites, named after Zaid, grandson of Husain, son of the Caliph 'Ali, but the Sunnis considered them heretics, like all Shi'ites. The Zaidis had converted many inhabitants of the southern Caspian seacoast, had extended their influence south of the Elburz Mountains, and were prominent in the region of Ray.

It is interesting that at Damghan they met a missionary of the Zaidi heresy who was openly making converts at that time. The group members concealed their identities in a large caravan they took to Nishapur, which had just been liberated from Zaidi control, to avoid being seized by Zaidi partisans who ruled the district of Damghan, as Togan explains (Togan 1939, xxi–xxiii). The Caliph was unable to control much of western Iran, for heretical movements were flourishing there. Apparently the backlash against those missionaries had barely begun, for shortly thereafter they were persecuted and the Samanid government supported a counter-missionary effort of Sunnis.

In Nishapur the Zaidi general Laila ibn Nu'man had held the city for three months until he was defeated and killed by the Samanids, by the commander of the army of Khurasan, Humuwayh Kusa, who is mentioned in other sources as Humuwayh ibn 'Ali, the military leader who secured the throne for the young *amir* Nasr ibn Ahmad in Bukhara. It is clear that Caliphal authority was challenged in many parts of Iran and Iraq, and the Samanid armies had to restore Sunni and Caliphal control of Khurasan. Even though the ruler Nasr toyed with heretical beliefs, perhaps as a counter to the influence of both powerful courtiers and Sunni religious leaders in his domain, the Samanid army put down heretical movements. Nasr, however, was forced to abdicate because of his religious leanings and died in 943.

The road from Sarakhs to Merv was the normal route from the Iranian plateau to Central Asia, mentioned by other geographers writing in Arabic. Merv was a large oasis with many villages and was famous for its textiles; it was a great trading center on the route east. Qushmahan, which no longer exists, was a small town at the edge of the oasis of Merv where the desert began, which had separated the old Sasanian Empire from Central Asia. The ruins of Amul, however, can still be seen today near Charjui on the Amu Darya in Turkmenistan. Across the river the voyagers came to the *ribat* or burg of Tahir ibn 'Ali, whose identity is unknown. The term *ribat* was originally used for castles or strongholds where Muslims gathered to make raids against nonbelievers to the east and north, but by the time of Ibn Fadlan it meant a caravanserai, or halting place for couriers of the state.

Mausoleum of Mir Sayyid Bahram (Samanid era), Bukhara oasis

Baikand or Paikand was an important commercial center, as excavations have revealed. Next they entered Bukhara, which probably meant the large oasis of Bukhara. The principal town was Numijkath, but it generally was itself called Bukhara (meaning "flourishing" or "endowed") after the oasis.

Bukhara always vied with Samarkand for pre-eminence in Sogdiana. Usually Samarkand held the distinction of principal city, and only under the Samanids did Bukhara become the capital of this dynasty. Even though Bukhara was out of the way for anyone coming from Charjui en route to Khwarazm, the embassy had to pay respects to the Samanid ruler and secure his aid in furthering their plans.

Al-Jaihani, the chancellor or vizier of the Samanid ruler, was known for his practice of questioning the travelers he received for information, which he then gathered into a geography book that became the primary source of knowledge about Central Asia for Muslims in succeeding years. He surely questioned Ibn

Fadlan about his observations on his return trip or obtained a manuscript of his travels. Al-Jaihani was a great patron of poetry and the arts, as well as an admired administrator.

In 918 Ibn al-Furat, the vizier of the Caliph, was removed from his post and imprisoned, and all of his property was confiscated. In searching for funds to pay for the embassy, including salaries for the teachers and judges who were to accompany the expedition, the estate of Ibn al-Furat in distant Khwarazm was chosen. Although we are not told, it appears that Ahmad ibn Musa had bought the confiscated estate and was to collect the revenues from it when he came to Khwarazm and turn them over to the embassy. But the bailiff of Ibn al-Furat, al-Fadl ibn Musa, remained loyal to his deposed master and kept the revenues. Instead of obeying the order to turn over funds to Ahmad ibn Musa, he sent messengers to intercept Ahmad and place him under arrest (under what pretext is unknown). Ibn Fadlan could not await the outcome of the quarrel between the two men. He had to continue on his trip without the money, which later caused trouble from the king of the Bulghars.

It is of interest that al-Fadl was a Christian, indicating the tolerance and trust of a Muslim official for a non-Muslim subordinate. We do not know what kind of Christian al-Fadl was; Central Asia at this time was home to Dyophysite Nestorians (members of the Church of the East, as they are called), Monophysite Syrians (or Jacobites), and followers of the Greek Orthodox persuasion, and any one of these groups could have claimed al-Fadl as its member. The fact that he had an Arab name may suggest a Jacobite connection, but with the existence of Khwarazmian trade connections with the west as far as Byzantium, he may have been Orthodox. There is no way to be sure.

The embassy spent three winter months, from December though February, in Khwarazm enduring great cold, which helped persuade the Muslim learned men and teachers on the expedition to abandon the embassy and return to warm

Baghdad. Jurjaniya, later called Urgench, was the main town involved in trade with the Turks of the steppes. This three-month lull should have been enough time to obtain the expected money; the fact that they did not appears to indicate either the freedom of action (or inaction) of underlings or the inability of the government to enforce its authority in many areas. Perhaps the government in Bukhara did not wish to interfere in affairs of Khwarazm, where the bailiff al-Fadl may have had enough influence with the local ruler to ignore any order of the Caliph.

The nature of the missing money itself also poses a puzzle. The text refers to four thousand Musayyabi *dinars*, but as far as I know gold coins called Musayyabi never existed. Perhaps our author means that the equivalent of four thousand gold *dinars* in Musayyabi *dirhams* was to be received. Since there were no gold coins at this time except medallions or commemorative coins, it seems plausible that the equivalent weight of gold in local *dirhams* may be what is intended. Or it may be only a slip on the part of a copyist.

At this time in Central Asia (Khwarazm, Bukhara, and Samarkand) several kinds of *dirhams* were in circulation, one of which was called Musayyabi, but all of these were different from the silver *dirhams* minted by order of the Caliphate. The former were struck in debased silver with the busts of pre-Islamic rulers, such as the "Bukhara king" (called Bukhar-Khudah in Arabic sources) in Bukhara—a practice that had long vanished in other parts of the Caliphate. In the oasis of Bukhara the coins were called Ghitrifi, and in Khwarazm they were known as Musayyabi *dirhams*. The local name for those *dirhams* that still bore the portrait of a pre-Islamic ruler, however, was *tazija*. The Islamic names of the coins probably were derived from earlier governors or viziers who approved their minting in the ancient format. The coins were valid only locally or in trade with the Turks on the steppes, who appear to have accepted the Musayyabi coinage of Khwarazm in their dealings with the

Silver coins of Nezak and other rulers in Northern Afghanistan, 8th–9th century

Khwarazmians. A third kind of similar coins were the Samarkandi, possibly the same as the Muhammadi *dirhams* of other sources. The Khazars, on the other hand, had a different monetary system. The moneychangers, like those throughout history, not only exchanged money but also sold dice and other objects.

The laws of supply and demand influenced the exchange rates between the local coinage and the silver specie of the Caliphate. At times when the output of silver coins was excessive, their value sank in relation to the local, debased coinage, for the latter then functioned as modern coins, whereas the silver coins had simply the value of the metal in them. But the relative values fluctuated. As long as the Samanids were powerful, the local coinage was highly valued, but after the fall of the Samanids a shortage of silver changed the picture. The Rus and the Bulghars, however, accepted only silver coins as specie in their realms, which suggests that we are dealing with equivalents in value of so many Musayyabi *dirhams* (that is, the equivalent of so many silver coins).

Khwarazmian merchants established a mint in the land of the Volga Bulghars and struck copies of Samanid silver *dirhams*, with a similar weight of 4 plus grams. By Samanid silver coins, I mean Caliphal issues that were minted by the Samanids, but valid elsewhere in the Caliphate. For smaller units, the silver coins were broken into halves or quarters, examples of which have been found in excavated hoards in northern Russia and in Sweden. (Since Ibn Fadlan does not mention this, it is possible that the mint was established after his trip.) In the eleventh century, however, the supply of silver dropped precipitously, as did trade, partly as a result of the expansion of new nomads over the steppes of Central Asia and Russia, going from east to west. Why the supply of silver dried up remains a mystery.

It is odd that the king of the Bulghars sought Musayyabi coins instead of the silver *dirhams* that were current in Russia, especially in trade with the Rus. Either the king needed the coinage of Khwarazm to pay persons from that land who were in his service (or to trade with the Oghuz or the Khwarazmians), or Ibn Fadlan is confused, meaning real *dinars* or rare gold coins. It is possible that the value of the Khwarazmian coins had risen to such an extent that they were now preferable to silver coins, but that surely would have been the case only in Khwarazm or among the Turks, who were trading partners of the Bulghars.

Remarks on Khwarazm

Yaqut's section on Khwarazm contains additions to Ibn Fadlan that are briefly mentioned here. When Ibn Fadlan speaks of Khwarazm, he means two things: the land of Khwarazm, and also the capital of the country, called Kath. When he speaks of the distance between Khwarazm and Jurjaniya, it means either the distance to the southern border of the country or to the cap-

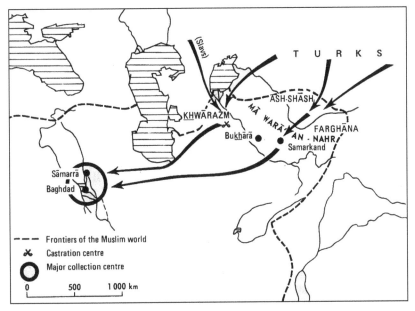

The trade in Turkish slaves

ital; it is difficult to say which. The shortest and best way to travel to Khwarazm was by boat on the Amu Darya, which was the means by which our group traveled.

The fur trade with the north was especially important for Khwarazm. Khwarazmian tailors made jackets and coats from sable, marten, fox, beaver, ermine, and weasel skins. Khwarazm was also the principal market of the slave trade for the Caliphate, and the Turkic tribes provided a steady supply of prisoners and children whom they sold to merchants or government officials. The practice of using slaves as bodyguards, or even as soldiers or officers, was a continuation from pre-Islamic times in Central Asia. In Baghdad, as elsewhere in Islamic lands, slave soldiers frequently became more powerful than other officials and determined policy. The best known such institution of slave soldiers was the corps of Janissaries in the Ottoman Empire.

The intense cold of the land made a great impression on the travelers from warm Baghdad, and our author dwells overly much on the cold, although he also mentions the existence of learned men in Khwarazm. Yaqut also says that Ibn Fadlan exaggerated in his descriptions—for example, by claiming that the Amu Darya river froze completely to the bottom, when we are told that the inhabitants made holes in the ice for their drinking water. It is uncertain how much of the material in the section on Khwarazm from Yaqut comes from Ibn Fadlan, for he was by no means the sole source of information on Khwarazm, although he was the main source in later Arabic works for the sections on the Rus and the Bulghars.

The Khwarazmshah, holding an ancient title, was really a governor of the Samanids, and he was upset that the embassy had not followed proper protocol through the Samanid *amir* from Baghdad. His motives in trying to dissuade Ibn Fadlan and his comrades from continuing on his journey are unknown. His accusation against Tekin seems to have been a lame excuse to conceal his real objections, as a young servant such as Tekin hardly could have had access to the Caliph, or even to his ministers, to play a trick to influence the embassy. The Khwarazmshah may have genuinely feared that he would be held responsible for any disaster that might have befallen the embassy in the land of the Turks. Also, he may have been influenced by the counsel of his courtiers and merchants, who suspected that their dealings with northern peoples might be upset by outside interference.

Although the Khwarazmshah in the end aided the embassy, some Khwarazmians probably had misgivings about the political aim of the embassy to conclude an alliance with the Bulghars. The Khwarazmians were influential at the court of the king of the Khazars, as well as having relations with the Bulghars. They may have thought the new embassy might upset their trade relations with both. Furthermore, they constantly raided the Oghuz Turks, who were enemies of the Khazars. So politics were at play, even though this is nowhere stated in the account of Ibn Fadlan. From Kath, the capital, the embassy continued on the river to Jurjaniya, which was the main town engaged in trade with the Turks.

Ibn Fadlan's remarks about the Khwarazmian language reflect what little we know about the written language, which has a complicated grammar compared to the Persian tongue that replaced it. We assume that Persian had become the medium of communication between different linguistic groups in Central Asia by the tenth century. Arabic remained the official language of government, but Persian was spoken in government circles, while Sogdian and Khwarazmian were rapidly disappearing except in villages. The common folk never learned to speak Arabic but did adopt Persian; later, with the expansion of the Turks, Persian gave way to Turkic tongues among the people. Persian remained the written language in Central Asia almost to the present, and it is still spoken in some cities and villages of Uzbekistan, as well as in Tajikistan.

It is impossible to identify or clearly describe all of the articles of clothing that the travelers donned to protect themselves from the cold. Some had special features of design or used special kinds of cloth or skin. It is difficult to picture the various items of clothing worn by the travelers, for the words used by Ibn Fadlan may refer to garments with which he was acquainted that were only similar to what he found in Khwarazm. The amount of clothing worn against the cold was excessive, but necessary for anyone coming from warmer climes. For discussions of the meanings of the various garments, refer to the notes of Togan and Kovalevskii.

The skin boats procured for crossing rivers on the voyage were probably similar to the coracles in use on the Tigris at Baghdad, but they must have been of considerable size to hold four or five men plus baggage. Spring was the time when rivers overflowed, as the voyagers found out in the difficulties of crossing the many rivers on their trip. Because of the distance they had to travel, it was necessary to leave Khwarazm early to have enough time to accomplish their mission and return before winter came. They did not wish to spend the winter in the land of the Bulghars. Furthermore, they only had to deliver the letters and gifts and give advice about Muslim practices, so a long stay in the north was unnecessary.

The Turkic tribes

There are questions about the descriptions of the customs of the Turks encountered on route to the Volga. How much did Ibn Fadlan exaggerate, and what did he actually witness, rather than just hear from others? Also, in comparing what he reports with similar accounts in later authors, one must always ask whether the later information was in fact derived from Ibn Fadlan's account, rather than from the geography book by al-Jaihani or other sources. For example, similar but fuller reports of punishing a person by tying him between two bent trees and then allowing them to release, thus tearing apart his body, are found in several later sources, as well as being attributed to the Mongols. Yet one wonders how widespread the practice was. Obviously, for a strict Muslim, many practices of the nomads must have appeared not simply lax but offensive. On the other hand, Ibn Fadlan could have refrained from reporting whatever offended him rather than registering his disgust at the conduct he describes.

Several times in the text Turks are described as laughing in their response to questions, and the relaxed and tolerant attitude of nomads toward the more regulated customs and mores of settled folk unsettled our author, who was, as a strict Muslim, repelled by what he regarded as the loose character of the Turks. The copying of Arabic Muslim formulas by them was especially annoying, since it indicated to him that the Turks were making fun of Islam and did not believe in what they pronounced, which of course was true. One may view the discussion among the Oghuz about what to do with the embassy (whether to plunder or to kill them) in the same light, for the discomfiture and fear among the embassy members probably amused the nomads, who were aware of the way they were viewed by settled people of the south. Ibn Fadlan's rigidity, and his apparent lack of a sense of humor, would be a natural target for mischievous Turks.

The Oghuz traded with, as well as raided, the Khwarazmians as a matter of normal nomad/settled relations, but with the Khazars they were enemies as well as competitors in trading. The Khazar state contained nomadic tribesmen as well as settled people, and the Oghuz were a threat to Khazar hegemony on the steppes to the east of the Volga. Previously, in the middle of the ninth century, the Oghuz had been allies of the Khazars in attacks against the Pechenegs, driving them west. Politics in the north was ever-changing, and today's friends might be tomorrow's enemies.

The marriage customs of the Turks our group met were widespread among other tribes on the steppes, as well as among the Mongols. The marriage of the son with the many wives of his dead father (except his own mother) was another widespread custom, probably necessary to keep together an extended family, and also having shamanistic influences. The hospitality of nomads, even to their enemies, was also extensive, while the Turkic means of slaughtering livestock ran counter to the Muslim practice of slitting the beast's throat.

The various Turkic titles reveal the complexity of rule among the Turkic tribes, for some were honorific while others were positions of real power. Double kingship was a feature of the Turkish tribes of Central Asia, and we see the importance of an assembly of a tribe's leading members in making decisions. Some tribal societies, such as Arab and Baluch, give unquestioned obedience to their leaders, while others, such as Turkish tribes and the Pashtuns, with their *loya jirga*, rely on consensus of the tribe. The freedom of the Central Asian tribesman to contradict his chief was surprising to outsiders.

Double kingship was superficially like the division of the Roman Empire under Diocletian, with two *augusti* and a *caesar* under each of them, but the members of the Turkic foursome exchanged places when a *khaqan* died. The number four may have had similar meaning for the Bulghars with their four sub-kings.

Of special interest to our traveler were the burial customs he noted. The customs of burying a chief with his possessions, and of placing the corpse of a Turk in a house before covering it with earth and then killing his horses, have been corroborated by excavations of kurgans (mounds) on the steppes. Frequently the corpses were placed in a sitting position. The erection of statues, usually stone but sometimes wooden, called *balbals* by the Turks, was also a widespread practice among the nomads of Inner Asia.

The Pechenegs, a Turkic people, had been driven west of the Volga almost to the Balkans by the Oghuz and the Khazars, and Ibn Fadlan only briefly saw a small group of them who had remained behind. We must remember that information came through a translator who himself may not have properly understood what he saw or was asked. The phallus in the cult of the Bashkirs most likely was a totem, perhaps of an ancestor, which was carved like a penis. The various gods of the Bashkirs also may well have been various totems of different tribes, while the story of the cranes that gave victory is found elsewhere among the nomads of Central Asia.

Further itinerary of the trip

Since the caravan went north of the more direct route to the Volga, probably to avoid the Khazar domains, they may have been breaking new ground on a lesser-known route. The rivers crossed have been tentatively identified as follows. (The modern equivalents of the river names in the text are suggestions; the reader may check them on a detailed map of the region.)

Text name	Contemporary river name
Yaghindi	Zhayindi
Jam	Emba
Jakhish	Saghir
Udil	Oyil
Ardin	Zhaqsibay or Kaldygayti
Warish	Olenty or Kaldygayti
Akhati	Ankaty or Buldurti
Ubna	Utba
Jayikh	Ural
Jakha	Chagan
Azhin	Irgiaz or Talovka
Bajagh	Mocha
Samur	Samara
Kinal	Kenel
Sukh	Sok
Kunjulu	Kundurcha
Jaramshan	Chirimshan
Uran	Uran
Uram	Urem
Baynakh	Mania
Watigh	Utka
Jaushir	Aqtay or Gausherma
Itil	Volga

These identifications are a composite of the suggestions of various authors in the bibliography.

The Bulghars or Saqaliba

The section on the Bulghars, called Saqaliba, is interesting and unique. The etymology of Saqlab (Arabic plural Saqaliba) is disputed, although many claim it is related to "slave," which is supposedly the origin of Slav. In the general usage of Arabs, this name designated the various peoples of central and northern Russia, whether Scandinavian, Slav, Ugrian, or Turkic, but for

Ibn Fadlan the term meant primarily the Bulghars. This suggests that the kingdom of the Bulghars included representatives of all the peoples mentioned. The language of the king and his court, however, probably was a Ugrian tongue related to Hungarian, for the latter had been neighbors until they left for central Europe (mainly under pressure from the Pechenegs and/or Khazars). Later, however, the Bulghars of the Volga adopted a Turkic language, such that today they are called Tatars of the Volga.

We do not know whether the acceptance of Islam by the king of the Bulghars was primarily political, in opposition either to the local pagans and the Varangians, or to the Kievan Rus and the Judaism of the Khazar court. There does not seem to have been a story about the king's making a choice of religions, similar to the tale about the choice of Christianity by Vladimir of Kiev in 989. On the other hand, it is possible that the neutrality of Judaism as a political force, as opposed to Christianity and Islam, had a great influence on the choice. In the early tenth century, there were few Christians in Russia, yet the Bulghar king must have been aware of the role of religion in the two great powers of the time, the Byzantine Empire and the Caliphate. The former had been allied to the Khazars, although by the tenth century ties had loosened. So it appears that two political axes formerly had existed: the north-south Bulghar-Caliphate alliance and the east-west Khazar-Byzantine alliance. Trade surely was an important feature of each alliance, but we have no sources directly testifying to the importance of trade in politics of the period. The sacking of Sarkel (the second city of the Khazars on the Don River) by Prince Sviatoslav of Kiev in 965 forecast an end to the Khazar kingdom and opened the steppes of south Russia to various nomadic tribes such as the Polovotsi.

The king of the Bulghars may have been called "ruler of the Saqaliba" in the translation of his title for the embassy with the intention of impressing the Caliph that he was a mighty ruler over all the peoples of the north. The four rulers or sub-kings under him may have had some symbolic significance, similar to the four generals of the late Sasanian Empire (according to the points of the compass: general of the north, east, etc.). Likewise, four was a symbolic number for rule over the four directions of the earth by Turks and Mongols. (The strewing of coins over the head was also a widespread custom, extending beyond the Turks to Russians and others; today it is even done over brides at weddings.) Inasmuch as it only took three days to gather the sub-kings and courtiers to the place of assembly, they cannot have been far from the court of the Bulghar king. The assembly was meant to impress the envoys of the Caliph with the power and influence of the Bulghar king, as well as to introduce everyone to Islamic protocol features.

The Bulghars on the Volga were both agriculturists and pastoralists, but trade was the main source of their wealth and the basis of the king's power. At the time of our author's visit the Bulghar king was in the process of uniting various tribes under his authority, but opposition existed. The people called Suwaz, who may be identified with the present-day Chuvash, apparently did not accept Islam or the authority of the Bulghars and moved away from the area close to the central Bulghar realm. Earlier, on the steppes, there lived a people called Sabirs (who may have been the ancestors of these Suwaz, if we read the final r for z). Others have suggested that the name should be read Suwar, referring to one of the towns or districts of the kingdom of the Bulghars and having nothing to do with the Sabirs. The confusion of final r and z may result from different dialects.

Another group of people mentioned in Ibn Fadlan's account were the Baranjar, who had converted to Islam. These may be the same as the Balanjar of the north Caucasus region, mentioned in certain sources; exactly when they moved north into Bulghar territory is uncertain. The mixture of tribes along the Volga, Finno-Ugrian as well as Turkic, makes a differentiation between them most difficult. Added to these were the Slav tribes and the Rus. It should also be mentioned that the northern people were called Majus in some Arabic sources, such as Garanati. Majus (magi) was the term applied to the Zoroastrians by the Muslims, who considered them fire-worshippers. Although we have no evidence that fire played the same symbolic role in the animistic religions of the northern peoples as it did for Zoroastrians in Iran, Arab authors may have used it as a general term for those who in some way honored the elements, including fire.

In any event, Ibn Fadlan was concerned with both the customs of the Bulghars and the institution of correct Islamic practices among the people. His gift of a black cloak and turban to the king was appreciated, for the king knew that black was the special color of the 'Abbasids and thus was a sign of comradeship with the Caliph. The failure to bring the money which al-Fadl ibn Musa had kept for himself, however, soured relations between the Bulghar king and the visitors, especially for Ibn Fadlan, the Arab leader of the group. Although the king and Ibn Fadlan became reconciled, the coolness toward others of his group may have induced Ibn Fadlan to depart earlier than planned and return the same way he had come.

Togan states that Yiltawar was the Bulghar pronunciation of the general Turkic title Elteber (Togan 1939, 105–6). He also gives detailed notes on other titles such as Kudarkin and Yanal. According to Togan, the name Wirigh of the ruler of Suwar (or Suwaz) was also a Bulghar pronunciation of the Turkic title *buyruq*. The influence of the titles of the Turks, which proclaimed them as warlike masters of the steppes, spread to their neighbors; even the Rus adopted the title *khaqan*. Since the Bulghar king was a vassal of the Khazar *khaqan*, perhaps in this case Tekin, the translator for Ibn Fadlan, may have used the subordinate Turkic title as the best way to explain a native Bulghar Uralic title. Given the Bulghar king's pride in his own worth, it seems questionable that he himself would have used a subordinate title of foreign origin among his subjects.

Although the king heeded the advice of our author in matters related to the Islamic religion, he could not ride roughshod over the leaders of the Muslim prayers throughout his domain if they had different ideas about rites and practices. This was revealed in the question of the number of times to recite the invocation to prayer from the pulpit. The double recitation of the *khutba* at the court of the king of the Bulghars was a feature of the Hanafi school of Islamic law, as opposed to the Shafi'i single recitation, which was the practice of the court in Baghdad. At first the king accepted Ibn Fadlan's request to have it recited only once; then, either in annoyance with him over the money he had not brought or in response to opposition from some of the religious leaders in his realm, the king asked Ibn Fadlan whether a double recitation was allowed. After receiving a positive answer, he ordered the recitation twice. As Togan states, the more liberal Hanafi position on what was allowed and forbidden in Islam was preferred by the Turks and Bulghars to the more strict Shafi'i school (Togan 1939, 49). Furthermore the Khwarazmians and others in Central Asia followed the Hanafi rites, and the Muslims in the realm of the Bulghars followed the Central Asians rather than others.

When our author departs from the narrative of events at the court of the king and turns to marvels in the land of the Bulghars, we leave his eyewitness account for a mixture of what he saw and heard from various persons, some of whom may have been tellers of tall tales. His description of the long days and short nights at the beginning of summer, and the change to a reversal of times by the time of his departure, is essentially believable, in spite of the criticism of Josef Markwart (1923). His description of the northern lights as clouds of jinn warriors fighting, however, brings in fancy. The barking of dogs as a sign of a coming year of fertility and good luck is found among other peoples of Inner Asia, who viewed the howling of wolves as a fortuitous sign. The descriptions in Ibn Fadlan's story of snakes, berries, and apples in the land are all convincing.

The drink made of bad wheat in marriage feasts of the Bulghars may well have been what is today called *boza* in

Turkey and elsewhere. Any drink that had alcohol and produced drunkenness was abhorrent to Ibn Fadlan, yet the various kinds of drinks made from honey or grain interested him such that he recorded information about them. The practice of obtaining the sweet sap of a tree by making a hole in the trunk and collecting the sap in a bucket is similar to the making of sugar maple syrup in New England, but the tree in the land of the Bulghars was not a maple.

It is difficult to believe that a rhinoceros existed in the forests of north Russia at this time. (Do we have here the fanciful story of a unicorn in the land of Gog and Magog, or does the story told to Ibn Fadlan refer to a kind of elk?) The shooting of game with arrows from trees, however, is well attested in the forests of the north. Tales of the fabled land of Gog and Magog were current in Medieval Europe and in the Near East. They derive from the fanciful story of Alexander the Macedonian, who drove savages to the north and built a wall to contain them, where they remained a threat to the world because of the danger they might break out of the wall. Some have sought a reality behind the story in the building of the Great Wall of China, but tales of the land of Gog and Magog also refer to the strange customs of their inhabitants. The origin of the name itself is disputed.

The burial custom of men mourning the dead and whipping themselves in contrition is a pre-Islamic practice in Central Asia, not related to the Shi'ite rites of self-flagellation at the time of Ashura (mourning for the death of Husain, son of the Caliph 'Ali). The practice of men cutting their faces with knives is attested both in literature and in wall paintings. The freedom of the women of the Turks, and the common bathing of men and women among the Bulghars, shocked Ibn Fadlan, though he noted at the same time that adultery was severely punished by people of the north.

The remark that the king of the Bulghars wrote to the people called Wisu raises the interesting question of whether he wrote in runes, or in Arabic with a translator to carry his message.

Runes existed in the north from Scandinavia and Hungary to Mongolia, but it is uncertain whether they were in daily use or used only for inscriptions or epitaphs. It is noteworthy that the Arabic alphabet used by the Tatars of Kazan was the same as that of Khwarazm, with three dots under the *sin*, for example.

Zaqariya Qazwini, a later author of the thirteenth century (cf. Markwart 1924, 300) says that the Bulghars bring swords from Islamic lands to the Wisu, where they are much prized. The Wisu were neighbors of the Jura, not mentioned by Ibn Fadlan, but it is hardly possible to identify either people with present Samoyeds, Voguls, or Ostiaks in northern Russia. The customs that the grandfather of a boy raises him more than his own father and that the brother rather than the son of a dead man assumes his inheritance were prevalent among many tribes on the steppes.

Almish, the Bulghar king, lived only a few years after the departure of the embassy and was succeeded by his son Hasan, who went on the pilgrimage to Mecca. The country of the Bulghars became the center of Islam and Islamic learning in the north, and it remained so until recent times. In 985 Prince Vladimir of Kiev raided the land and occupied the town of Bulghar for a short period. Afterwards, fighting between the Bulghars and various Russian princes finally ended in the conquest of Bulghar and its incorporation into the great Russian state, but that was much later, in the mid-sixteenth century under the reign of "Ivan the Terrible," and after Kazan had replaced Bulghar as the main town of the region.

The Rus

Much has been written about this portion of Ibn Fadlan's story. James Montgomery (2000) gives notes about the text, especially on the controversy over whether the Rus were only Swedes or a mixture of peoples engaged in trade with Bulghars and Khazars. Probably the Rus were mostly Scandinavians with Slavs and Finns joined to them over the course of years of settlement in today's Russia, but the number of newcomers from Sweden probably was always small in relation to the native Slavs and Finno-Ugrian-speaking inhabitants.

Sometimes the words "Viking," "Varangian," and "Rus" are used interchangeably, but the first term was applied mainly to those Scandinavians from Norway and Denmark who behaved like pirates rather than merchants. (The word "Viking" probably is related to the Old Norse *vik-*, meaning "inlet" or "waterway," rather than to the Latin *vicus*, "market," although it may be a conflation of the two.) The Rus or Varangians, on the other hand, were primarily traders, although not averse to plunder. Attempts to differentiate between the two designations have led nowhere, so we may consider the two as synonyms. It should also be mentioned that today the Finns call the Swedes "Ruotsi" after Roslaget, the old name for the province of Uppland where the old town of Uppsala was located, while Russians are called "Vännen," from the Slavic tribe of Wends.

The Rus had come to the east in the eighth century and had established themselves in Lagoda in the north as their principal settlement, but they later transferred to Novgorod. Then they moved south on the Dnieper River, and Kiev became their main

Medieval depiction of Vikings building Novgorod

town. As early as 908, they raided Constantinople across the Black Sea. By the time of Ibn Fadlan's trip, the Rus had been well established in Novgorod, Kiev, and elsewhere, so those who came to the Bulghars to trade may have come from any Rus settlement (although those described by Ibn Fadlan, we may guess, came from the north down rivers from the Baltic). Those already settled in towns such as Novgorod probably would not have been so wild and uncultured as our author depicts them. Although they were mostly traders, these Rus were notorious for their raids and pillage of the settlements of peoples they encountered.

In the first half of the tenth century, the Rus descended the Volga; that is, they made a portage from the river Don, called the river of the Rus, to the Volga and into the Caspian. According to Muslim authors, in 913—eight years before the voyage of Ibn Fadlan—a large raiding expedition of the Rus, described as a branch of the Saqaliba, descended the Volga River into the Caspian Sea and raided its southern shores, plundering and burning houses. The people living in Gilan and Tabaristan were fearful of these raiders, who came with the aid and blessing of the Khazar *khaqan*. News of the booty and slaves secured by the raiding Rus, as well as the destruction of homes and property, must have reached Baghdad, and thus could have been a factor in the dispatch of an embassy to the Bulghars.

After the voyage of Ibn Fadlan, the Rus again raided the southern shores of the Caspian, and especially Azerbaijan, where in 944 they seized the town of Barda'a. The geographer Mas'udi describes this invasion in some detail. This raid of the Rus made such an impression on the inhabitants of Azerbaijan that the poet Nizami of Ganjeh (writing in Persian, with much fantasy, in his *Iskander Nameh*) relates how Alexander the Macedonian fought the Rus and confined them behind a wall. Thus the Rus for some time became bogeymen in the eyes of the inhabitants of the regions they had devastated.

Some scholars have considered the description of the Rus as

tall, blond, and always carrying axes as evidence that Ibn Fadlan was speaking of Swedes. But these two features, as well as the tattoos, could also fit Finnish and Slavic tribesmen. Likewise, the large bladed swords were widespread in the west, including among Germanic tribes. The ornaments worn by the Rus women impressed Ibn Fadlan, although he considered the colored ceramic beads in their necklaces—which the women especially sought and valued highly—to be rather ordinary. Large numbers of such beads have been found in graves of the period, testifying to our author's true observation (Jacob 1887, 145–46). These beads apparently were not made by the Rus, but most likely were imported from southern lands. One instance of a change in the text I owe to A. I. Samarrai, who proposed that the passage describing how the Rus prized the beads, translated by others as "which are on the ships," should be "which are formed on the polishing stone" (reading *yakawanu 'ala al-sufuni* instead of *yakunu 'ala al-safani*). This reading, I suggest, makes more sense than simply having beads on their boats.

Although the clothing, jewelry, and arms of the Rus interested him, our author was even more observant of and disgusted by the Rus practice of washing in a basin rather than having flowing water poured over hands and face as the Muslims would do. The presumed superiority not only of the Islamic religion, but also of Islamic practices and customs, over others makes the remarks of our author similar to the attitudes of many European travelers of the nineteenth century in Africa and Asia. Muslim ablutions and washing of the hands were contrasted with the uncleanliness of the Rus.

Apparently the Rus were frequent visitors to the trading center of the Bulghars; otherwise they would not have had their own houses and images of their deities. On the other hand, it is difficult to identify practices that Ibn Fadlan observed with those in Viking-age Sweden. By this time, the Varangian Rus in these regions had adopted local customs, such as the offerings to the wooden figures, and adapted them to their own traditions.

This practice, as far as I know, has not been reported in Scandinavia.

Muslim authors inserted fanciful tales in their writings to interest their readers, and it is difficult to know how much to believe. Some information may be genuine or only somewhat exaggerated. For example, Mirkhond, a fifteenth-century historian who wrote in Persian, reports that a custom of the Rus was to leave all of their possessions to their daughters after death. They give nothing to their sons except a sword to each, saying, "This is your part of the heritage" (Fraehn 1823, 58–59). This sounds more like an attempt to show the ferocity and warlike nature of the Rus than actual practice.

Among the customs of the Rus, the funeral rites made the deepest impression on our author, and Ibn Fadlan goes into detail about what he saw and what was explained to him by a translator. He may have imported into the description Islamic ideas of paradise as a verdant garden where a dead person would meet relatives who had preceded him. The nakedness of the man who brought the first lighted stick to the funeral pyre could be interpreted as a sign of great mourning, while placing his hand over his anus may have meant to protect himself from evil spirits entering him in the time of weakness without clothes. Again this is not reported elsewhere.

The combination of a boat funeral with cremation seems to have been the developed practice of the Varangians in the east at the time of the embassy. Previously, either interment in the ground, cremation, or a boat funeral was common practice. The funeral of the prominent Rus was elaborate, with many rites, all of which had to be explained by an interpreter who rarely would elucidate on the cultic significance of them (which he may not have understood himself). One can only speculate about the meaning of such matters as the killing of a dog, a hen, and horses. Apparently not only the girl to be sacrificed, but also the mourners, drank mead until they were intoxicated. The mound for the ashes and the erection of a mound over the spot

The fur trade in martens and sables, as depicted by Olaus Magnus

were typical features of a Viking funeral, but they are also similar to the mounds and memorials of a dead Oghuz Turk chieftain, also described by Ibn Fadlan.

The Rus used 'Abbasid and Samanid silver *dirhams* as their
currency, breaking the coins if they need a half or fourth as a
payment. Apparently the Khazars, as well as the Bulghars, minted copies of the Islamic coinage, but the former also had their
own coinage, although it is uncertain what other coins the
Khazars minted. Probably all silver coins would have been
accepted in the markets just for their weight and silver content,
if not for any other value assigned them. Several sources,
including Garanati, have suggested that Russian princes used
furs as a monetary medium. From the large quantity of seals,
usually in lead, with marks or *tamgas* on them found in excavations in Russia, it would seem that there was some sort of control over the use of skins and furs by merchants in the domains
of the Russian princes. This is an unresolved issue, requiring

more research into the mercantile, taxation, and monetary practices of various Rus principalities before their absorption by the
principality of Moscow. Given the great importance of furs of all
kinds in the trade with the south, however, it would not be surprising if furs played a role similar to coinage for the Bulghars,
the Rus, and others in the northern lands.

The Khazars

Ibn Fadlan's account of the Khazars is all derived from
hearsay, but information about them is so scarce that even his
remarks are significant. The Khazars have been the subject of
great interest because of the conversion of their king and nobility to Judaism, the second such event after the conversion of the
royal house of Adiabene in northern Mesopotamia at the beginning of the Common Era. The Khazar kingdom was a union of
a number of tribes in a confederation after the invasion of the
Avars and Turks in the middle of the seventh century, just when
the Arabs were expanding in the south. At first their homeland
was south of the Caucasus, but after the Arab invasion the center of their rule became the northern Caucasian steppes, with
their capital at the mouth of the Volga River, a strategic place for
control of trade. Their language originally seems to have been
related to the Uralic Bulghar tongue, but it became Turkic soon-
er than the Bulghar language did. This linguistic element came
to predominate in the union of peoples comprising the Khazar
khaqanate. In essence, however, the Khazar realm was a multi-
linguistic as well as a multi-ethnic state.

The expedition of the Arabs against the Balanjars, part of the
Khazar realm in the Caucasus region north of Derbent on the
Caspian coast, began a series of conflicts between the Arabs and
the Khazars. The Arabs took Derbent in 662, but struggles continued until 737, when the Khazars gave up their capital at
Samandar (on the plain of the northern Caucasus more exposed
to Arab raids) and moved their capital to Itil on the Volga. Their
attention now shifted to the north, and the ninth century saw an

extension of their influence to the west as far as Kiev, which was said by some to have been founded by the Khazars around the year 820. Their second most important town was Sarkel on the river Don, founded ten years later.

About the year 700, the ruler and his court converted to Judaism. The reason and circumstances of this conversion are unknown, though the presence of many Jewish merchants in the capital may have been a factor. Although there were pagans and Christians among the subjects of the Khazar ruler, the Muslims became the majority by the end of the kingdom. The Khazar ruler's support for religious leaders and judges of all the faiths in his realm indicates his tolerance in matters of religion. It is reported that in 861 a debate between Christians, Jews, and Muslims took place, with no group favored. Possibly this was an attempt to mimic similar debates which had occurred at the court of the liberal 'Abbasid Caliph Ma'mun in Baghdad.

The Khazar state expanded to the north and west in the ninth century, from the Don and Dnieper rivers to the Ural in the east, and the Bulghars became their vassals. The Pechenegs and later the Oghuz were enemies of the Khazars, while the Magyars moved west out of their control. As noted, relations with Byzantium were close, such that a Khazar princess in 732 was married to Constantine V and became Empress Irene; their son Leo, who succeeded to the throne, was called "the Khazar." Relations with Byzantium did not always remain friendly, however, when the interests of the two powers clashed, especially in the Crimea and western Georgia.

At the time of Ibn Fadlan's trip, not only had Khazar ties with the Byzantine Empire dropped, but Khazar relations with the Rus had also deteriorated. This breakdown in relations was especially marked after Rus ships returned from raids against Islamic lands south of the Caspian in 922, when the Muslims in the Khazar capital Itil (called Sarighshin in some sources) attacked the Rus with the acquiescence of the *khaqan*. The Rus, however, continued their raids on the Caspian, so trade and the promise of booty must have revived cooperation between them and the Khazars for a time. Vassals of the Khazars, including the Bulghars, had already declared their independence in 965, when prince Sviatoslav of Kiev, together with Oghuz allies, dealt a mortal blow to the Khazars' empire, paving the way for the ultimate breakup of the kingdom and the dispersal of its peoples.

The *khaqan* had assumed a kind of elevated, sacral character, such that an underling called Khaqan Beg, who himself had an assistant with the Hungarian title of Kundu(r), managed the affairs of his kingdom. The dual kingship and hierarchy of posts was a feature of Turkic tribal states on the steppes of Central Asia and seems to have existed among the Khazars as well.

As with other groups, the burial customs of the Khazar rulers fascinated Ibn Fadlan. The powder spread over the tomb of the ruler, mentioned in the text, was probably meant to eliminate the decay and smell of corpses. The sending of a river over the tomb of a ruler is recorded in various contexts, the most famous being the burial of Alaric the Goth in Italy after his conquest of Rome. How much of what our author reported about the harem of the ruler, and the awe in which his subjects regarded him, was true or distorted is impossible to determine. The general picture, however, is confirmed by other sources.

The destruction of a synagogue in Dar al-Bubanj has been variously identified with Pumbedita (a Jewish center in Mesopotamia), a synagogue in Spain, or one in the southern region of the Khazar domains. There is no way to determine its location. The Khazars were scattered and became only a little-remembered folk, like other ephemeral peoples of the Russian steppes.

Aftermath of the embassy

Was the embassy of Ibn Fadlan successful in its objectives? Let us examine the goals of the mission in order. The call to the Oghuz to accept Islam fell on deaf ears, for on the return trip the chief of the Oghuz did not accept the invitation in the letter from

Nadhir al-Hurami. Only later did Islam expand among the Turkic tribes of Central Asia. The Bulghar king did not receive the money promised him, and the fortress he wished to construct was not built. Close ties with the Caliphate were not established, since the Bulghars rather maintained and strengthened trade—and perhaps political ties—more with Central Asian Turks and Khwarazm than with Baghdad. Also, the position of Muslims in Khazar domains suffered some repression and decline, although this did not last.

The members of the expedition also did not gain from their trip. On the contrary, they remained in the bad graces of the Bulghar king, and they may have blamed their leader Ibn Fadlan for his enmity toward them. The latter did not succeed in converting the Bulghars from the Hanafi to the Shafi'i school of Islamic practices and law. In the end, even his book was forgotten, although excerpts from it were made by others writing about the north. No manuscripts of his account have survived, which is why the Meshhed manuscript was touted as unique, but it too was part of a later compilation.

Several years after the voyage, and before the death of Caliph al-Muqtadir in 932, an embassy from the Bulghars, headed by the son of the Bulghar king, did arrive in Baghdad on the pilgrimage to Mecca. According to Mas'udi, the source for this information, only the gifts—especially the black furs from various animals of the northlands—aroused any comment. Not one word was mentioned about the voyage of Ibn Fadlan, and one may wonder whether he fell into disfavor after his return. In a sense, the trip of the new Bulghar king was an answer from the Bulghars to the trip of Ibn Fadlan, even though Mas'udi does not mention this.

What happened afterwards in the north? In 985 Vladimir, prince of Kiev, raided the land of the Bulghars and destroyed their capital. This was followed by more raids and counter-raids, besides fighting between the Bulghars and the Russian princes, now more Slavic than Scandinavian. The successors of the Khazars on the steppes of southern Russia were the nomadic Polovotsi or Cumans, a Turkic-speaking people, who dominated the entire steppe area and fought against the Russian princes.

There was apparently a massive movement of tribes in the eleventh century, both in the Near East, with the Oghuz and their rulers the Seljuk sultans, and on the steppes of the north. In effect, one finds a "nomadization" of the western Asian world, from the time of the fall of the Samanids at the turn of the millennium until well after the Mongol invasions, which also changed the face of the whole eastern world.

Today in Poland among the Karaim Jews, who reject the authority of the Talmud, are some who claim descent from the Khazars, but this claim cannot be substantiated. On the other hand, since the Karaim, or Karaites as they are called, flourished in Mesopotamia and Iran before the time of Ibn Fadlan, their missionaries may have converted the court of Khazars, and after the fall of the kingdom some may have spread westward. Unfortunately we are uncertain about the Jewish beliefs of the Khazars.

The successors of both the Volga Bulghars and the Khazars were the Mongols, who established a state known as the "Golden Horde." Russia was ruled by the Mongol Khans for almost three centuries. After Mongol rule crumbled, the Russian rulers of the principality of Moscow became their heirs, as well as inheriting their rule over the many peoples who occupied the vast lands of the steppes and the forests. While the Tatars of Kazan today rightly claim descent from the Volga Bulghars, many other ethnic groups contributed to the populations along the Volga River. Ibn Fadlan introduced us to this world.

APPENDIX A

Other Muslim Accounts of the North

A qadi in his tent

The Strange Things of Creation by Qazwini
(cf. Markwart 1924, 300)

The inhabitants of Bulghar bring swords from Islamic lands to the Wisu. They are swords that have no pommels or decoration, but they are taken as they come from the fire and are put in water and hardened such that when [the blades] are hung from a cord and stroked by a finger, a ringing is heard.

Then every sword is brought to the land of Jura, for the inhabitants of Jura pay a high price for one, and they throw it into a dark sea. When they do this God causes a fish to come out of the sea, as large as a great camel, and they eat from it. [This fish story is found elsewhere, including a version in Ibn Fadlan.]

The *Tufhat al-Bab* of Abu Hamid al-Mazini al-Garanati
(or Granati) (cf. Dubler 1953)

A century and a half after the voyage of Ibn Fadlan, a traveler from Granada, Spain, visited Eastern Europe and left an account of his travels in Arabic. A translation of the section on the Bulghars follows. (The chief town of the Bulghars is also called Bulghar.)

Bulghar is a large town, all constructed of pine, but the city walls are of oak. Around the town are various nations, extending without limit to the seven climes. When the day is long it is twenty hours, and the night is four, but in winter it is the reverse. In summer at noon it is hot, more than anywhere, but at night it is so cold that one has to wear many clothes. I was there in the month of Ramadan in the summer, and fasted underground in a house where there was a spring of water.

In winter the cold is excessive, such that wood splits from the frost. But the king, at this time of great cold, goes on raids against the infidels, and takes in captivity their women, sons and daughters, and horses. The people of Bulghar are the most hardy of people regarding the cold, while their food and drink is principally mead, which is cheap.

In their land are the bones of the tribe of 'Ad; the width of a tooth of them is two inches and the length four. From the head to the shoulder is five meters and the head is like a huge mound. Many remains are there.

Under the earth are tusks like an elephant's, white as snow and heavy as lead, one of which is a hundred pounds in weight, more or less. They do not know to what kind of an animal it belongs. They send it to Khwarazm and Khurasan, where they fashion combs and boxes and other things from it, just as they carve elephant tusk. But this is stronger than elephant tusk and does not split.

There are many peoples beyond their land who pay taxes to the Bulghar king. The meaning of the word bulghar is "wise man." That is because a Muslim merchant came from Bukhara, and he was a doctor of law who knew much about medicine. The wife of the king became ill, and the king too was very sick. The medicine that they took did not help, and both were near unto death. The Muslim said to them: "If I treat you, and you are cured, will you accept my faith?" Both said yes to him. He treated and healed them, and they accepted Islam.

The king of the Khazars came at the head of a huge army and fought with him [the Bulghar king], and said to him: "Why did you accept this religion without my permission?" The Muslim said to him [the Bulghar king]: "Do not fear; say, 'God is great, God is great; praise God and bless Muhammad and his family.'"

The [Bulghar king] attacked and put the enemy force to flight, such that the [Khazar] king concluded peace with them and accepted their faith, saying: "I saw huge men on white horses who attacked my army and put me to flight." The Muslim said to him: "Those men were the army of God, great and merciful."

Since a wise man is called *bular*, consequently they called the country Bular, meaning "wise people," and the Arabic of that was changed to Bulghar. I read that in the History of Bulghar, written by a Bulghar judge, who was a student of Abu al-Masali Juwaini, may God bless him.

There is a place [near Bulghar], the inhabitants of which pay taxes [to Bulghar]. Between them and Bulghar is a month's journey, and they are called Wisu. There is another region called Aru [Udmurtia?], and in it they hunt beaver, ermine, and a kind of squirrel. A day there in autumn is twenty-two hours. They bring from there very fine beaver pelts. The beaver, it seems, is an animal that lives by large rivers. It builds its home in a plot by the river and makes for itself something like a high bench, and to the right of it steps for females. Under that bench is a place for himself, to the left a place for his children, and in the lowest part of that house a place for his slaves. The house has a door facing the river and another door a little higher on the bench. They feed on the birch tree and fish.

They attack one another and take one in captivity. The merchants in that land and in Bulghar single out the pelts of the captive beavers. The reason for that is the beaver slave cuts the birch for its master and drags it with its mouth. The servant that cuts the tree puts it on its shoulders and shakes off the hair of its skin, right and left. For this reason they say, "That is the slave of a beaver, and the beaver which serves thus has no hair on its skin."

He continues, writing about the Jura and their land, and he has more about Kiev and the Hungarians, and he also uses the term Majus for the Saqaliba.

Commentary

Abu Hamid Muhammad ibn 'Abd al-Rahim al-Garanati al-Andalusi was born in Granada in 1080, and after studying Islamic law and other Islamic subjects he embarked on long voyages to Cairo, to Baghdad, and finally to Saksin near the mouth of the Volga, where he remained twenty years teaching and acting as a missionary to the Pechenegs. In 1149 he went to Bulghar and the following year he visited the Rus and Kiev. He continued to Hungary, where Pechenegs and other nomads of the steppes had gone. In 1162 he was in Mosul, where he wrote his book of travels, and after seven years he went to Syria, where he died.

He relates his tale about the bones of giants to the people of 'Ad described in the Quran, and his remarks seemingly about the tusks of mammoths may in fact be about the ivory of walrus or narwhals. It is possible that his story of the curing of the royal couple of Bulghar, and their acceptance of Islam, may be true. Certainly by the time of Garanati's visit the power of the Khazars had been broken, and that of the Bulghars had increased. Also, Islam held sway in the domain of the Khazars after their loss of rule and the decline of Judaism. The account of the beaver is unique although laced with imagination. In both accounts of the northlands, by Ibn Fadlan and Garanati, fact and fiction are mixed, though the latter predominates with Garanati. Nonetheless, compared with other medieval writings in both east and west, these two may be considered as quite sober.

APPENDIX B

General Remarks on Nomads and Conversion

Frequently, simple and obvious aspects of a subject are neglected or forgotten. For example, in the division between nomads and settled folk in Central Asia, another category has been ignored: that of pastoralists. Pure nomads, who seek only better pasturelands in their movements, are rare in history, the Mongols being perhaps the best example. Pastoralists, by contrast, were those who sought to migrate to settled areas, or to exist adjacent to them and in symbiosis with settled folk, and they seem to have been more numerous than true nomads in the past. Invaders of settled lands were usually pastoralists who knew about the riches and advantages of rule over agriculturists. Nomads, on the other hand, raided and then retreated to their natural habitats, or else they sought to destroy or change tilled fields into pasturelands. Anthropologists tell us that pastoralists and agriculturalists were akin to each other and that change in the manner of life existed in both directions, with settlers becoming pastoralists and vice versa, although the usual pattern was for pastoralists to settle rather than the reverse. Here we shall term the society of the pastoralists, or nomads if we put them together, as tribal as opposed to the settled people, even though tribal divisions may have persisted among the latter.

Two themes have dominated the history of Inner Asia: trade and water, especially in irrigation. Trade was important for nomads and pastoralists alike, while water was the lifeblood of farmers or peasants. Central Asia (the southern part of the larger Inner Asia), although it had mountains, was primarily a land of oases surrounded by deserts. Sometimes the oasis could expand with irrigation, such as Bukhara, Samarkand, and Kashgar, but a constant fight against encroaching sands was the lot of all of them. Inasmuch as each oasis was a self-contained unit, the formation of a centralized state over many of them was rare and usually was possible only with outside intervention from China in the east or Iran in the west. Trade with pastoralists or nomads was of great significance to the inhabitants of the oases, and usually a mutual arrangement of hegemony or protection by the former over the settled people insured peace. When an ambitious chief of tribes, or a ruler in China or Iran, sought to expand his control over the oases, then conflict would arise.

There were significant differences between the "steppe" and the "sown," as we may term the struggles in history between a state built on the union of mobile tribes and one that ruled over settled folk. These differences, with some exceptions, may be described as follows:

1. The military force of the tribe or tribal confederation was based on all of the able-bodied or fighting men (the horde), while the kingdom or empire had a professional army. This difference is evident in ancient Iran of the Achaemenids, when the initial tribal forces (Old Persian *kara* or German *Heer*) were later transformed into an army (Old Persian *spada* or German *Armee*). Before the invention of firearms, an army of settled people was often at a disadvantage in conflict with mounted warriors who could attack and retreat with a speed and mobility unmatched by their opponents.

2. Fundamental differences existed in the mode and consequences of conquest by the steppe and the sown. Tribes conquered by confederating each other, or by applying the same

principle to the settled people they ruled. This is best observed in the institution of the mawali, or clients, of Arab tribes at the time of their expansion in the seventh century, but it also applied to the inhabitants of the oases of Central Asia when they were conquered by horsemen. When a king or emperor conquered other lands, however, he sought to expand his own domain by taking over the government or bureaucracy of the conquered state and incorporating it into his own kingdom.

3. The institution of the ruler was different in the two areas. For the tribes, the individual ruler was important, with his ability to hold the allegiance of various clans and tribes. If his son or successor was capable, then continuity would ensue, but it depended on his qualities of leadership. This could be termed the charisma of the individual. In a kingdom of settled folk, however, it was the institution of kingship that insured continuity. One might characterize this as the charisma of office rather than of the individual.

How was continuity insured in a kingdom? Usually it was through the sacralization of traditions of rule, for religion was vital to the continuity of rule. The end result was the establishment of a state religion or church, which provided the spiritual support for rule. For tribes, on the other hand, religion was unimportant, and charismatic clans in a tribe provided the continuity of rule, which in any case was always fragile and subject to change. This meant that steppe empires were usually ephemeral, lasting only as long as the clan or extended family of a tribe retained a charismatic hold over all of the tribesmen. The most famous and long-lasting of steppe dynasties, of course, was that of the Mongols under Chinggis Khan.

4. If we examine the art traditions of the tribes of the steppes, on the whole we find what may be called folk art (that is, art made by the common folk). The art of the empire, as might be expected, can be designated as imperial art, either ordered by the court or copied for the nobility. The art remains of the Achaemenids, of the Sasanians, and even into Islamic times, are

Mongols setting up camp

"high" art by professional artists. Folk art, of course, also existed in settled areas, but little has survived and it too was influenced by styles of the court. The same was true in China, where
professional artists created objects for the court or the entou-
rage. Styles of art varied in both realms, but the art of the people of the steppes reflected their lifestyle. The importance of the
horse and the camel is evident in decorations of their accou-
trements, such as bridles and saddles. Furthermore, nomads
favored vivid colors, such as the reds and yellows in their carpets and textiles. The motifs in their arts always have been highly stylized, rather than realistic.

5. Finally, as mentioned, trade was vital for tribal life, and
merchants on the whole were respected, if not honored, in
steppe society. Merchants brought luxuries to the tribesmen,
and both silk from China and silver from Iran were treasured.
On the other hand, traders were not well regarded either in
Chinese or in Iranian societies, although their importance grew
as both societies began to realize the value of trade for their

economies. Merchants, however, never attained the rank and respect that landowners and courtiers held in both China and Iran.

These differences between the steppe and the sown throughout history should be kept in mind in assessing the interactions between peoples. Today in Inner Asia one could characterize a continuation of the steppe or nomadic traditions as a "rural" or "tribal" mentality and the traditions of the sown as an "urban" mentality.

Another topic of interest is writing, which gives us information about the past. One may forget that writing was highly specialized in the past and few people could qualify as scribes. Moreover, there probably were at least three types of scribes: royal or governmental scribes who kept records for the government, religious scribes who copied religious texts, and scribes for the common folk, merchants, and the like. Until recently, professional scribes used to sit outside the post offices of Kashgar, Kabul, and Tehran, where they would compose and copy letters for customers. And, as in the past, the scribes were also translators who could write in several languages.

But there is another question one must ask, and that is: what kind of language are we discussing? I long ago proposed a scheme (Frye 1974, 64) for understanding different languages at all times and places, which may aid us now. One should distinguish the following languages, even though in many cases they may fall together as one tongue. First, we have the "official" written language, which is that of the court or administration; then there is the "official" spoken language, which at first sight may be the same as the former but usually is not. Third is the language of religion; fourth, a dialect spoken at home; and finally, a language of trade and commerce, which again may be the same as the first or second or may be a *lingua franca* different from all the above.

Let us examine several cases in the past. In Bukhara in 922, the time of Ibn Fadlan's trip, the "official" written language of the city was Arabic; the "official" spoken language was Persian; the religious language was Quranic Arabic for Muslims, the Avesta for Zoroastrians, and Syriac for Nestorians or other Christians. The home dialect was Sogdian, probably by this time heavily influenced by Persian. The language of trade probably was Persian. If we go back half a millennium, what was the linguistic situation in Bukhara? The written language at that time was either Sogdian or Kushan Bactrian, if the Kushans ruled the oasis for a time; the spoken language was Sogdian; the religious language was Avestan for Zoroastrians; and at home a Sogdian dialect was spoken. Sogdian also was the language of international trade, although far to the east (in the oasis towns of Turfan, Hami, etc.), Chinese competed with Sogdian. This model can be applied everywhere—even in English, where a French-Latin vocabulary is used in writing, while a Germanic word is generally preferred in speaking.

Finally, we turn to religion and conversion. In East Asia and India, religion played roles different from the western Asian experience. Let us begin with the ancient Near Eastern world. In ancient Babylonia, Egypt, and elsewhere in the region, religion was locally based. This means that deities were numerous and they frequented large or small areas. Thus Marduk was the special god of Babylon, Assur of Assyria, Baal of Phoenicia, etc. Certain sites, such as a large tree or a spring of water, were the abodes of certain spirits or deities, and even a passerby would be advised to pay homage to a local spirit. If a Babylonian went to Egypt, he wisely would sacrifice to Isis or Osiris, while not forgetting to pay homage to Marduk in his own house. In other words, there was no impetus to convert in the present sense of the word.

In the Hellenistic world, after the conquests of Alexander, syncretism of Oriental and Greek forms of religion, as well as identification of local deities with Greek gods, grew in popularity. At first rulers came to be called saviors of their people if they were victorious in battle or defenders of their subjects against external attacks. Then ideas of mystery religions, in which an individual would be initiated in a group community, began to spread. Also, the memory of a world or universal empire of the Achaemenids, followed by the Seleucids, influenced the growth of a concept of a universal or world religion. A religion was universal if it was open to all and not restricted to any locality or tribe or people. But it was not until the third century of our era, after Caracalla granted citizenship to all in the Roman Empire in 212, that common self-identity in that empire changed. It was no longer a privilege to be a Roman citizen; rather, adherence to a cult or religion became the vogue, and allegiances changed. People came to be identified by their religion, and new attitudes arose.

Obviously, if one's beliefs were universal, they must be true for all times and places. The natural corollary followed: if one believed in the absolute truth of his faith, then others who did not adhere to that religion must be persecuted. Intolerance replaced tolerance, and new concepts of orthodoxy and heresy came into being. Christians were the fanatics of the day in both the Mediterranean and Near Eastern worlds, and they prevailed. Not only were followers of other religions or cults converted or persecuted, but orthodoxy also imposed, by law, a system of beliefs, rituals, and practices. Religion of the state was born, and as a government would not tolerate rebels, so also the church would tolerate no deviations. We know about early Christians suffering persecution, but after the triumph of Christianity we do not hear of others being persecuted by Christians. They just disappeared.

In the first century of the Islamic conquests, ideology reverted in some degree to ancient concepts. The Arab tribes believed that Islam was an Arab religion, restricted to tribesmen and their clients. To become a Muslim meant to become an Arab: to break with one's previous community and faith, learn Arabic, and become part of the Arab community, the *ummah*. In the early years of the Umayyad Caliphate, instances of refusal to accept

Viking ruler of Kiev accepting Christianity

converts are recorded, since doing so would have reduced the capitation taxes paid by non-Muslims. It was only after the establishment of the 'Abbasid Caliphate in 750 that conversion to Islam became more widespread. This is not to deny the previous missionary work of pious Arabs, especially the Caliph 'Umar II, but on the whole no great efforts were made to turn the entire population into Muslims under the Umayyads.

In Iran this wave of conversions reached its crest when competition with heretical missionaries of the Fatimid Caliphate in Cairo, spreading the Ismaili heresy, changed the scene. This accelerated movement to convert began shortly before the time of Ibn Fadlan's journey, and his expedition may be viewed in this light.

Competition also influenced the conversion of peoples outside of the Islamic world, and Russia was a prime example of this competition. It is known that the Varangian princes of Kiev, and of other towns in Russia, accepted Greek Orthodox

Christianity, while the Bulghars accepted Islam. It is not my intention here to discuss the details of both conversions, but rather to focus attention on the methods and aims of an earlier conversion. One of the earliest, if not the earliest, examples of the conversion of a king and his court to one of the world or universal religions was the conversion of Queen Helena of Adiabene, with its capital at Arbela (Erbil), and of her two sons, Monobazus II and Izates II, to Judaism around the year 50 of the common era. This was before the revolt of the Jews against Roman rule and the destruction of the temple at Jerusalem, and the question arises: what happened to cause this conversion? Unfortunately, we do not have detailed information about the conversion and can only speculate. Could competition between Judaism and the new Jewish heresy of Christianity have induced missionaries of Judaism to launch a counter-program of conversion? Whereas Christian missionaries seem to have worked among the masses, it appears that the Jews saw an advantage in persuading royalty and aristocracy to convert, hoping this would persuade their subjects to follow suit. In any case, among the principalities of Mesopotamia a fertile field existed for conversion from ancient, outdated, and ineffectual faiths (in the eyes of new converts).

Perhaps Judaism became a model for the east, for in the early third century Mani also contacted the royal court of Shapur son of Ardashir the Sasanian, with the hope of making conversions to his new religion. He did convert the Sasanian prince who was governor of Mesene, in the delta of the Tigris and Euphrates, and hoped to influence others. It appears that his efforts provoked a reaction of the Zoroastrian priests at the court, and they were not amiss in establishing fire temples in lands conquered by Shapur (cf. Gignoux 1971). With the establishment of Christianity in the East Roman (Byzantine) Empire and Zoroastrianism in the Sasanian state, missionary activity apparently diminished, if at times it did not cease. With the coming of the Arabs and Islam, gradually both Christianity and Zoroastrianism were relegated to minorities in virtual ghettoes, and conversion was limited to Islam, except in frontier areas such as the Caucasus. In a case strangely similar to Adiabene's, the ruler (*khaqan*) of the Khazars and his courtiers accepted Judaism about the year 740 (cf. Golb and Pritsak 1982). According to Ibn Fadlan, Judaism was still the faith of the rulers in his time, although later Islam took over the realm.

One may ask whether conversion to another religion, usually considered a personal matter, in the past had a political as well as a spiritual goal. (This question does not include the Muslim fighters for the faith, sometimes fanatic, called *ghazis*, in Spain, Anatolia, and eastern Turkistan. They were matched by Christian counterparts best known for their heroes—the Cid in Spain, Diogenes Akritas in Anatolia—and by a Uighur Buddhist, possibly called Budrach, against the Muslim Qarakhanids of Kashgar.) Surely the mission of Ibn Fadlan to the Bulghar ruler on the Volga River had political ramifications. What were they? Following the saying that the enemies of my enemy are my friends, the Caliphate saw the Bulghars as allies; hence, the journey of Ibn Fadlan, as we see in the text and commentary to it.

APPENDIX C

Byzantine and Iranian Commercial Rivalry

Although the Byzantine Greeks regarded their Sasanian enemies through centuries-old glasses fashioned by Herodotus and other classical authors, the Persians had lost most of the records of their past by the third century C.E. When Herodian (VI.2), as well as other authors such as Dio Cassius, assumed that Ardashir, the first Sasanian ruler, intended to restore the empire of Cyrus and Darius, this historian of the Roman emperors was only drawing on his own knowledge, and not on the presumed memory of the Persians for their own past.

The latter, however, were not completely ignorant of their past as many scholars have assumed. Rather, they had two accounts. One was a fragmentary knowledge of the Achaemenids and their successors; another, more popular and widespread, belief was in the epic nature of their past, probably developed primarily by the Parthians, based on the Avesta, sacred book of the Zoroastrians. Most inhabitants of the Sasanian Empire seem to have retained a tradition about their former glory and grandeur, with a belief that once they had ruled most of the civilized world. So their pretensions to rule were more of an epic, or almost divinely ordained, nature, than a right based on the reading of history books. It is, I believe, a fundamental difference between the Byzantine and Sasanian Empires, so alike in other matters, that the Byzantines had read their Herodotus and Thucydides, whereas the Persians had not—indeed could not—read their Behistun inscription or other native writings, which had not survived. The names of Cyrus, Cambyses, and Xerxes may have been known to elites, but they surely were not common knowledge among most people.

The epic view of history that the Persians held had probably been brought to them from eastern Iran and Central Asia during that little-known period of Iran's history from Alexander to Ardashir. I should like to characterize this period as a kind of nomadization of Iran, somewhat comparable to the Jahiliya (ignorance) period of Arabia's history before Muhammad, when another nomadization occurred. For the effects of the invasion and spread of the Parthians over the Iranian plateau, and the expansion of the Sakas and other nomads in eastern Iran, profoundly altered the history of all of Iran. As a result, Iranian society was permeated with ideas of chivalry and "feudalism," if we may use this term in its widest connotation and not in its western European meaning. The Sasanians were the heirs of this feudal society, which later authors writing in Arabic called the age of the *muluk al-tawaif,* or "tribal kings." It lasted throughout the Sasanian era, although later the centralized bureaucracy of the Sasanians in many ways came to usurp the influence and power of the feudal lords

Even before the Sasanians, the Zoroastrian leaders of the clergy were important, but during the reign of Shapur II (309–379 C.E.), their influence increased, as they felt threatened by the spread of Christianity and sought more authority at court. Even though we have no direct evidence, it may be proposed that the Zoroastrian religious leaders promoted their Avestan, epic view of the ancient history of Iran as the official account of the past, supported by the government, while western views were rejected. An indication of this change is found on coins, where the epic title of *kai* (Avestan *kavi*) regularly appears under Yazdegird II (439–457) and later.

In the building of a bureaucracy, the Sasanians borrowed much from the Romans and, later, from the Byzantines. After all, the Roman Empire was the only available model from which the Persians could borrow, if they had to borrow at all, and further-more it was a worthy, prestigious (though hated) model. In spite of the warfare between the two empires, they did respect each other as the two great representatives of the "civilized world." For both empires, India and China were too far away, and too exotic, to play any role on the stage of history to the west of them—extending from the Mediterranean to the plateau of Iran. This feeling of respect, mixed with enmity toward the enemy, dominated relations between the two empires throughout their history until the Arab conquests. Indeed one might suggest that with the fall of the Parthian state and the rise of the Sasanians, and with the transfer of Roman power from Rome to Constan-tinople, the medieval age began in both the eastern Roman state and Iran. The protagonists in the east-west struggle were now much more evenly matched than in the days of Trajan and Hadrian. This contributed to the mutual feeling of respect that the two empires seem to have had for each other, as found in sources such as Theophilactus Simocatta.

Most scholars would agree that the relations between the two empires changed from the third to the seventh centuries, as did the ideologies of the two states, as found in the Byzantine author Petrus Patricius. I hasten to correct any impression that the two empires were any less antagonistic; rather, they reached a kind of balance of power. In the sixth century, as contrasted with the fourth and fifth centuries, the Byzantine emperor Justinian (527–565) and the Sasanian Shahanshah Chosroes I (531–579) changed the military, commercial, and diplomatic relations between the two empires. Justinian's revival of a vassal king-dom of the Arabs on the desert frontier was matched by a simi-lar development on the other side. Henceforth, almost until the rise of Islam, the pro-Persian Lakhmids and the Byzantine-

Detail of 6th-century Sasanian
silver bowl depicting the ruler Chosroes I
(Anushirvan) on the throne

supported Ghassanids were to play an important role in relations between the two empires. Furthermore, the defensive systems of the two empires were considerably strengthened, as we know from Procopius and from later Islamic sources on pre-Islamic Iran, which attribute to Chosroes the building of defensive walls (like the Roman *limes*) on both the northeastern and western frontiers of the empire. Just as Justinian was simply rebuilding and renovating older Roman walls and defenses, Chosroes, likewise, was not an innovator; for example, the Mesopotamian defenses previously had known the famous *khandaq Sabur,* or "ditch (and wall) of Shapur II," as it is known from Arabic sources.

This is not the place to discuss military changes in this period, including the expansion of espionage, and the development of new kinds of weapons, possibly including new kinds of swords. Nonetheless, it should be clear that the sixth century was a time of change for both empires. Diplomatic and commercial relations also evolved, and we now turn to them.

By the time of Chosroes I "of the immortal soul," as the Persians called him, the Christian threat to the state had passed, since the Nestorian Christians of Iran were as hostile to their co-religionists in Byzantium as only mutual heretics can be to each other. So the fear of collaboration with the enemy on the basis of religion, on the whole, was gone. On the other hand, with the consolidation of an "orthodox" Christianity in Byzantium came also a stabilization of Zoroastrianism, after the Mazdakite revolt, in the Sasanian Empire. The alliance of political and religious power in Byzantium, which one could almost call a theocratic absolutism, was matched by a counterpart in Iran. One may suggest that this polarity of political ideology in both camps created a modus vivendi in the sixth century, but political events led to a violent confrontation of the two ideologies in the seventh, with a consequent bitter anti-Persian propaganda at the time of the Byzantine emperor Heraclius, represented by George of Pisidia and other writers. The diplomacy of the sixth century had reached a high point of form, and of mutual concern, with the flight of philosophers in 529 from Athens to Persia, and their return at their own request, but with the support of Chosroes, a few years later. It is interesting to note that the Byzantine emperors regularly informed their brother Persian monarchs of the accession of a new emperor to the throne of Constantinople, and the Sasanian ruler did likewise with his parallel. This too changed in the seventh century.

In the realm of literature, the Sasanian *andarz* genre, or "mirrors for princes," flourished in the time of Chosroes I. Interestingly, we find the first real Byzantine "mirror" in Agapetus, deacon of the church of St. Sophia, in the time of Justinian ca. 530. There is no evidence for the translation of Byzantine "mirrors" into Pahlavi, or vice versa, but mutual influences were possible. Indeed, if one compares Agapetus, and others who write in this genre of Byzantine literature, with Middle and New Persian counterparts, the similarity of ideas is striking, even though one is Christian and the other is Zoroastrian. In both, the ruler is the center of the universe, the viceroy of God on earth, who stands between God and the ruled. Religion is identified with the social order, and justice is the maintenance of this order, which requires obedience from everyone. Incidentally, the Iranian ideals of kingship persisted long into the Islamic period of the history of the Near East, until in the eleventh and twelfth centuries al-Ghazali and others sought to Islamize the old Sasanian traditions that had persisted into Islam.

To return to the question of diplomacy in the sixth century, however, it should be remarked that although the various Christian sects were frequently at each other's throats, the Christians were still the best ambassadors between the two countries, and as a matter of course, Syrians, Arabs, and other people of Mesopotamia were the best intermediaries between Greeks and Persians. There was, it seems, a greater coming and going between the two empires than hitherto supposed, at least before the seventh century. The common picture of both empires was that of almost hermetically sealed domains, to be entered only by express permission of one or the other of the governments. Political and other refugees, however, were to be found on both sides, and the sources make frequent reference to them. Granted that the borders of both states were closely guarded and there was nothing approaching the mobility of modern times, still the evidence for interchange in the sources is, I believe, more than the usual opinion warrants.

This was especially true of Christians: Syriac, Arabic, or Armenian speakers on both sides, not to mention the native Greek or Persian Christians. For example, Mar Aba, a future catholicos of the Persian Christians, and himself a Persian convert from Zoroastrianism, was in Constantinople around 523. Paul the Persian was also for a time in the Byzantine capital. That Christians from Iran were active in Constantinople is proved by a Middle Persian inscription on a sarcophagus excavated in the Chaya district of Istanbul in 1964. The grave was that of Khordad son of Ohrmazafrid from Persia, who lived in Constantinople for one year in some capacity, possibly serving as a *boulleutes* or a mediator of some sort. The inscription most likely was engraved around 410, because the sarcophagus was found within the Theodosian walls, which were built at that time. Just what sort of duty this Persian Christian performed is unknown, but the very existence of the sarcophagus suggests that many similar cases of contacts between Greeks and Persians existed beyond those found in our sources.

One would expect the Christians also to have been active in the trade between the two empires. The strictures on trade on the Mesopotamian frontier, as outlined in the famous treaty of 561 between the Sasanian and Byzantine empires, are described in detail by Menander Protektor. The treaty between the two states continued to limit the number of towns on the frontier where trade between the two could be performed. There were no caravans coming from one land deep into the other; rather trade was limited to three frontier cities, and government restrictions on trading were prominent. Naturally smuggling was rampant on the frontiers, but confiscations and heavy penalties by both states made smuggling a great risk. Since transit trade also fell under these restrictions, it suffered greatly, as did trade between the two lands at the end of the sixth and beginning of the seventh century.

Because of these difficulties in commerce, and for other reasons, Byzantine merchants began to search for routes to bypass the Sasanian domains in their trade with southeast Asia, primarily for spices, and with China for silk. The story of changes in trade routes to the east from Mesopotamia to western Arabia (with the subsequent rise of the Hijaz and Mecca, as well as the attempts of the Persians and the Byzantines to control South Arabia, or Ethiopia) is a well-known and fascinating account of Byzantine-Sasanian rivalry in the Indian Ocean. The most outstanding feature of economic development in sixth- to seventh-century Arabia was the shift in volume of transit trade from Mesopotamia to the western Arabian route along the Red Sea. Likewise, the story of silk and the overland trade of Byzantium with China has long interested scholars. Less known, and somewhat neglected, is the Irano-Byzantine commercial rivalry in Russia, which paralleled the southern trade.

Sasanian coins, known as *drahms* or *dirhams*, were found in great numbers mostly in the Perm and pri-Kama areas, in the same region where the majority of silver bowls and ewers in Russian collections (both Byzantine and Sasanian) were excavated. The earliest hoard of Sasanian coins dates probably from the sixth century. Most of these coins, however, are of later date, together with coins of the 'Abbasid Caliphate. But it is significant that the earliest and most abundant finds of silver are from the first area in Eastern Europe open to Oriental trade. In this area, which probably was also the first region in the greater Russian area to develop a town life with markets, were found plates from various sources—regular Sasanian bowls and ewers, post-Sasanian silver objects (possibly even of local manufacture), and Islamic silver plates based on Sasanian models. Not only Byzantine bowls, but also silver plates from Syria have been found in the Perm area.

Why was such an amount of silver found in this area? First, I would relate the expanded commercial activities of the Sasanian and Byzantine empires, at the end of the sixth and throughout the seventh century and even later, to the "discovery" of northeastern Russia by merchants of both empires. Second, the products of this region, both luxuries and household goods, became much appreciated in both states. Honey, the sweetener of antiquity; beeswax; furs; and walrus ivory, more treasured than elephant ivory, came into prominence in the trade. The Persians seem to have had a greater predilection for furs than the Romans and Greeks, but the fur trade grew in importance in both the Byzantine and Sasanian empires. It is true that this trade greatly expanded only after the Bulghars moved north on the Volga, around 650, under pressure from the Khazars, and while the Arabs were expanding onto the Iranian plateau, but the impetus for this trade had started before this time. Third, the Byzantines, as well as the Sasanians, had to fight, conciliate, or bribe the northern barbarians who threatened their frontiers, and with what better means than silver, which was highly prized? Perhaps it may have been at this time that the gold objects of the Scythians and Sarmatians vanished and silver became "the currency of the steppes" up until the present. Finally, silver flowed to the north mainly because it fetched higher prices there than elsewhere. So drinking bowls, given as presents by Sasanian kings to their favorites, seem to have found their way to the north in considerable numbers.

The first imperial names or stamps to appear on Byzantine silver vessels date from the reign of Anastasius I (491–518), and this practice continued until the reign of Constans II (641–668). The reign of the former is almost parallel with the reign of Kavad, father of Chosroes I, in the Sasanian Empire, when many reforms and changes in Iran were initiated. It also coincides with the period when there was no regular silver coinage in the Byzantine Empire. Byzantine silver must have been turned into objects for trade and gifts, since during this period we have evidence of the widespread distribution of Byzantine silver objects. Silver spoons, for example, have been found in the Sutton Hoo burial of a Saxon chief in England, as well as in Syria, in the Caspian Sea provinces of Iran, and in Sweden and Russia. That silver vessels were highly prized everywhere is attested by objects with both Greek and Pahlavi inscriptions, such as a ewer in the Cleveland museum. Since the silver trade was so widespread and international in character, I suggest that the Sasanians copied the Byzantine practice in the notation of silver objects (there are no stamps on Iranian silver objects), and inscriptions engraved on silver vessels of Sasanian Iran are the result of such a registration. Thus the inscriptions can be used as a terminus ad quem, but not as a sure means of dating the objects, for most probably silver antiques and contemporary objects were registered at the same time.

That objects of different provenience, and possibly even different dates, could be found in one site has been attested by finds in Russia and Sweden. It should be added that not only the Byzantine and Sasanian merchants participated in the silver trade, but also the Khwarazmians, Sogdians, and Bactrians in Central Asia. A remarkable find at the site of Chilek, near Samarkand, in 1961 produced, among other objects, a Sasanian plate of Peroz, a Hephtalite plate, and a Sogdian plate and cup. The layer in the site from which these four objects came is dated in the early seventh century. We know further from the excavations of Panjikant, east of Samarkand (now in Tajikstan), that the houses of the fourth and fifth centuries were small and poor, whereas from the sixth and seventh century they greatly increased in size and richness, with a great abundance of wall paintings—testimony to the large commercial expansion of the end of the sixth, and throughout the seventh, century.

Thus, I believe one can characterize the post-Justinian and post-Chosroes I age as one of great economic expansion and enterprise, from the Indian Ocean to the newly opened Kama and Perm regions of northern Russia. The meaning of the change from the "gold standard" of the *Völkerwanderung* age to the "silver economy" of the Viking era in Europe, together with the silver and gold policies of the Byzantine and Sasanian empires, requires more study and more information. Suffice it to say that the rise of Islam in the south, and the entry into history of the forestlands of Russia, had a background in the economic history of the Byzantine and Sasanian empires after Justinian and Chosroes I.

APPENDIX D

Merchants in Inner Asia in Pre-Islamic Times

What was the ethnic and linguistic composition of Inner Asia before Islam? By Inner Asia, those interested in this vast area mean the Eurasian landmass from Gansu province in western China to the plains of Hungary in Europe, and from India to the Arctic Ocean in the north. Archaeology is our only source of information about this area in ancient times, since external Chinese and classical sources are frequently unreliable or difficult to understand. We are obliged to project backwards based on information from later accounts, and to interpret the sparse notices in all written documents, to reconstruct a picture of Inner Asia before the seventh or eighth century of the Common Era.

Aside from the Chinese and classical sources mentioned above, the overwhelming majority of preserved records are religious, but a few commercial writings and inscriptions have survived. The region known as Transoxania has yielded some inscriptions and coins, as well as letters, in the Sogdian, Khwarazmian, and Bactrian languages. The first two of these languages were written in alphabets derived from Aramaic, while the last used a modified Greek alphabet. Bactria, on both sides of the Amu Darya, was a rich agricultural region, described by Greek authors after the conquests of Alexander as a "land of a thousand towns." Trade and commerce was less important in Bactria than in Sogdiana and Khwarazm, two lands of oases. Bactrian merchants did go south to India in the wake of the conquests of the Greek kings after Alexander, but by the seventh century Sogdian merchants came to dominate the commerce of Inner Asia. Like the ancient Greeks and Carthaginians, the Sogdians established trading colonies far and wide. We hear of Sogdian colonies in Dunhuang and even in Changan (present-day Xian), as well as in Mongolia. They left their records in the Sogdian language wherever they went, and the Mongols and Manchus later adapted the Sogdian alphabet to their own languages. Sogdian merchants even carved their names on boulders in the valleys of the upper Indus River, in present-day Gilgit and Hunza.

Who were the native people with whom they traded? Probably by the first century of the Common Era, western Mongolia, which had been inhabited mainly by Iranian-speaking Scythian or Saka tribes, was being transformed into an Altaic (Turko-Mongol) domain by tribes moving from eastern Mongolia. The first fruits of the change to be noticed by the Romans occurred with the invasion of the Huns in the third–fourth centuries, but Hunnish tribes also moved south to India and the Iranian plateau. They also moved into western China (today Xinjiang), mixing with Indo-European–speaking Tokharians and, in the southern part of the Tarim Basin, with peoples related to Tibetans, as well as to the ancestors of the Burushaski speakers (now in Hunza). These people speak a language that, like that of the Basques in northern Spain, is unrelated to any other. Their geographical location, as well as old traditions among them, suggests that they once inhabited the southern rim of the Tarim Basin. Old Tibetan texts refer to a people called "Bru-zho" or "Bru-sha" northwest of Khotan, and it is possible they were the ancestors of the present Hunzakut, as the people of that mountain region are called.

There were also Iranians in towns such as Khotan and

Karashahr who began to write in their language, called Khotanese-Saka by contemporary scholars. The preserved texts of this language are Buddhist in content, for that religion was the first universal or world religion to make many converts in western China, and Khotan became a great center of Buddhism. In that language the word for merchant is "su-li," which is found in Tibetan as "sulig." In Chinese texts of the Tang dynasty (seventh through ninth centuries), the name of the oasis of Kashgar is "Su-le" or "Shu-li," so it is possible that all the words are related. The early Tang pronunciation of the name of Kashgar would have been something like "se-lek," which could be a variant of "Sogdik," the Sogdians' name for themselves. Inasmuch as the Sogdians were the most numerous merchants in Inner Asia,

Model of a Sogdian merchant from Astana tomb in Turfan, Xinjiang

we could postulate a derivation of the common noun "merchant" from the name "Sogdian" in both Tibetan and Khotanese-Saka. Thus, "Kashgar" would be "the town of merchants." Although one cannot prove the existence of a large Sogdian colony in Kashgar, this town was the logical center for Sogdian

trading activities in the east by virtue of its geographical location. In any case, Kashgar was the city of merchants par excel-
lence.

The later Chinese designation of the oasis of Kashgar as
"Kash" or "Kashi" may likewise reflect a connection with the
west, considering its similarity to the names of the Kashka River
and the town of Kesh in present-day Uzbekistan. It is possible
that the early Sogdian merchants who established a colony in
Kashgar came from Kesh and brought the old name with them.
The transfer of names from old to new locations can be found in
many areas in history, but demonstrating a connection between
these two names in particular must be left to future research.

I previously mentioned the religious writings, overwhelm-
ingly Buddhist, but there were also Manichaean and Christian
texts. The early Manichaean adepts were tenacious in their missionary activities, possibly inspiring other universal religions to
follow their example. Christians were also active in proselytizing their faith, and while Zoroastrians and Jews were more lax
in this regard, they were by no means averse to converts as they
became later. The Nestorian church, also known as the Church
of Persia or the Church of the East, sent missionaries to China
and India, who traveled with caravans much as Ibn Fadlan did
later on his voyage to the Bulghars on the Volga River.

Although Buddhism flourished in Bactria and in the east, it
was not popular in the homeland of the Sogdians. One may ask
why many Buddhist remains have been found or excavated in
Bactria, Kucha, and Khotan, while Kashgar and Sogdiana have
not yielded many remains of stupas (the dome-shaped structures used as Buddhist shrines) or of Buddhist paintings and fig-
urines. One possible answer might be that Sogdian merchants or
colonists, like the nomads with whom they traded, were generally tolerant about religions. With Christian, Manichaean,
Zoroastrian, and shamanist followers in their homeland, the
Sogdians did not devote themselves to one faith over others,
and they had no "state church" after the manner of the

Sasanians. As traders, they were pragmatic and preferred to spend their resources on large well-appointed houses, such as those excavated at Panjikant, rather than on religious structures or monuments. Buddhism was probably too unworldly a faith for active merchants. It is true that later, in western China, Sogdian translations of Buddhist texts were made. However, the translations were from Chinese, rather than from Sanskrit or another language, and may have been made only to please the Buddhist Chinese customers of the Sogdians. Teachings of repose and unworldliness had more success with people like the Bactrians, more bound to their soil, than with the active Sogdian merchants.

Trade over the Silk Road was of course two-way, but because of the great distances and slow transport, the commodities traded had to be expensive and rare, worth the great expense of caravans and security from bandits. Both products and ideas made their way from China to the Near East and vice versa. The main item from the east was silk, but other objects included paper, beautiful ceramics, and artistic bronze pots, as well as precious stones and metals. The slave trade was especially active, but little is known about this trade along the Silk Road. Sogdian merchants were middlemen for spices from India and the Near East, as spices substituted for refrigerators in antiquity. Carpets, silver plates, dried fruits, and many other objects were traded from the west to China. Berthold Laufer (1919) and Edward Schaefer (1963) have exhaustively investigated the items that went over the Silk Road, so their results need not be repeated here.

Coinage was important for merchants, and the "international" trade on the Silk Road led to the use of coinage in trade—the first sophisticated manner of exchange other than barter between peoples of different cultures. On the basis of the coins that have survived, one may ask what the relation of local copper coins to silver coinage was in Inner Asia. How did the Near Eastern practices of weighing silver coins, testing them by biting, and breaking them coexist with copper coins used in the contemporary manner of simply representing a value, and not for the content of the metal? To address this question requires a glance at the monetary situation in pre-Islamic times.

The Sasanian Empire maintained a high standard of purity in its silver coinage throughout the duration of the dynasty, more than three centuries (ca. 225–650). As a result, Sasanian silver gained a reputation for reliability among merchants, which was not shared by the debased silver coins with varying degrees of silver content minted in the oasis states of Central Asia or by nomadic rulers such as the Hephtalites. Farther east, Chinese coinage existed on a different basis. Generally speaking, Chinese cast coinage was fiduciary, while the Sasanian silver coins that circulated in the bazaars of Turfan, Kucha, and other cities were accepted because of their silver content (since the Sasanian Empire obviously had no control over those regions).

The study of ancient Chinese coinage presents many problems. For instance, it is not clear whether the market determined the value of copper or bronze Chinese coins, or whether local authorities proclaimed the relation of the coins to real property, such as sheep or goats. In the oasis cities beyond the western borders of China, the use of bronze or copper Chinese coins fluctuated with the rise and fall of central Chinese authority over the distant realms. But the silver coins too seem to have flourished and declined, almost disappearing after the fall of the Sasanian Empire to be replaced by bronze Chinese coins. Barter remained in use for various items, especially silk, which then became the main currency in the Turfan oasis and elsewhere. Events in China proper may have contributed as well to the declining use of silver coins in the markets of the oases. There is also controversy about whether silver coins were used as a commodity, based on the weight and purity of the silver, or as money in the modern sense. The answer may be that both uses obtained at different times and in different oases.

Little by little, as archaeology develops in China, more

Sasanian silver objects are being uncovered, including beakers and plates as well as coins. They may not equal the number found in northern Russia, but they show that trade in such objects was just as important in the east as in Russia. The Sogdians had almost a monopoly on long distance trade to China and Mongolia, and they were also active in the west, with a trading colony in the Crimea. The vogue for western products, especially exotic items such as ostriches, was especially popular in the early Tang period of China's history, and the Sogdians were not slow to supply the court at Changan with such rarities.

On the other hand, local trading certainly was much more widespread than international trade over vast distances traveled by one merchant. The Sogdians acted as middlemen, bringing objects from east to west and vice versa. For example, amber from the Baltic appeared in the treasury of the Shosoin in Nara, Japan, most probably brought through the intermediary of a Sogdian merchant. This merchant would not have gone all the way to Japan; objects such as amber were passed from one hand to another until they reached their final goal. The discovery of several sepulchers near Changan with Zoroastrian motifs carved on the stone suggests that rich Sogdian merchants were interred in them. This is not surprising; it again shows the importance of international trade and the need for trading colonies in the pre-Islamic period.

After the Arab conquest of Khwarazm, Sogdiana, and Bactria, there was initially a decline of international trade in Inner Asia. With the establishment of the 'Abbasid Caliphate and the rule of the Samanids, trade again flourished. The eleventh century, however, saw the expansion of Turkic tribes over the Near East and the oases of Xinjiang, which curtailed long distance trading. The strange disappearance of silver in Inner Asia at that time has not yet been satisfactorily explained, for much still needs to be done to elucidate the economic history of Inner Asia.

APPENDIX E

Byzantine and Sasanian Trade with Northeastern Russia

The history of the steppes of southern Russia has been viewed as a series of invasions of nomads from the east who displaced their predecessors, either annihilating them, absorbing them, or forcing them to move westward. Until the fourth century C.E., southern Russia was dominated by Iranian-speaking peoples: first by those generally called Scythians by classical authors, and then by the Sarmatians, with many divisions such as the Alans, the Roxalani, and others. After the Hunnish invasions, the Turkic period of steppe history began, for the interlude of the Goths and the movement of the Finno-Ugrian Magyars to the west were mere episodes in the overall development of this area's history.[1]

Unlike the Alans, who moved to the Caucasus area with the coming of Turkic-speaking peoples, the Iranians were not all displaced. Some of them remained in settlements in southern

---

1. It must be emphasized that the words "Turkic" and "Iranian" refer only to people whose rulers or the mass of whose population spoke a Turkic or an Iranian language. We know that tribes and peoples in Eastern Europe and Central Asia were highly mixed and under various cultural influences from the centers of civilization. We must use some general designations for lack of satisfactory terms, but the reader should heed the caveats regarding the history of the peoples of this vast area.

Russia, where they continued to trade and to spread their culture on all sides. It is my contention that the Iranians in the towns of southern Russia acted as middlemen in the trade between the Sasanian empire in the south and the Ugrian-speaking peoples of northern Russia. It is possible that the Sasanians enjoyed greater success than the Byzantines in their trade (and possibly in their diplomacy) with the peoples of the north through the efforts of their Iranian kinsmen in southern Russia. That the Sasanians were indeed more successful in trade than the Byzantines is indicated by the fact that Sasanian silver plates found in the Perm and Kama regions far outnumber Byzantine objects. Let us examine this area and adjoining regions, first to determine generally what has been found, and second to interpret the material remains.

The fact that almost all Sasanian coins discovered in Scandinavia and Russia have been found in hoards together with Islamic coins has led many scholars to assume that trade between Iran and eastern and northern Europe developed only after the establishment of the 'Abbasid Caliphate in the Near East. Although most evidence points to a great increase of trade in this period, especially with the expansion of the Vikings, there are indications that such trade existed in pre-Islamic times. The most significant evidence of early trade relations between pre-Islamic Iran and the Kama and Perm regions of northeastern Russia is the large number of fifth- to eighth-century Sasanian silver bowls found in these regions. By contrast, the comparatively few silver bowls older than these have been found only in southern Russia, in the Crimea and Saratov regions. It should be noted that finds of Byzantine silver vessels parallel the Sasanian ones, although on a smaller scale and with a wider distribution. We shall discuss this below.

General archaeological evidence of contacts between these areas is less convincing because of the difficulty of dating the strata. Nonetheless, one may presume that trading relations between north and south existed at this time, since there is plen-

Trade routes in the region of the Russian rivers

ty of evidence from both an earlier (Scythian-Bosporan kingdom) and a later ('Abbasid) period. Contacts may have been
broken during invasions of the steppes of southern Russia or
periods of internal problems, but these breaks may be viewed
merely as interruptions in a long period of continuous trade—
that is, as exceptions rather than the norm. The question we ask
is, why have silver bowls appeared in great numbers in the
Kama-Perm area, dating from the period of the last century of
the Sasanian empire into Islamic times? Obviously, this question
has two parts: why did the people of the Kama-Perm regions

want silver, and why did the Sasanians supply it?

The answer seems simple: silver plates were a good investment for the Ugrian-speaking peoples because they were small objects of great value that could be carried easily by merchants and exchanged with the nomads of the steppes (silver having always been the currency of nomads). The Kama-Perm peoples could obtain the plates in exchange for fish, hides, wax, honey, amber, and especially furs, which were prized greatly in Iran, though not so greatly in Byzantium. Another luxury article from the north was ivory from walruses and even mammoths, more highly valued in the south than elephant ivory for knife handles and other decorative uses. Thus, the motives for trade between these peoples are apparent. However, these same motives would also have existed in other areas where no silver objects have been found. Furthermore, the great number of silver objects in the Kama-Perm regions was not just a discovery of modern archaeologists; the old Russian chronicles frequently mention "silver from beyond the Kama," or "Kama silver," indicating that the people of this area were well known for their love and hoarding of silver.

The key to the problem of the large quantity of silver in the Kama area was provided by Russian ethnographers of the nineteenth century who investigated the religious practices of the forest peoples who were not Christians. They discovered that silver plates and other silver objects were used as part of the religious cult of the people who inhabited this area. Old Scandinavian sagas corroborate this finding. It is outside the scope of this article (and of the competence of its author) to discuss the religious practices of the inhabitants of the Kama-Perm regions, but the reason for the accumulation of silver objects in this area is clear. We may now turn to the other end of the trade route, the original home of the silver plates.

We have already mentioned the articles of trade sought by Iranians. We need not investigate the fur trade or ask why the furs were so highly prized in Iran—it is, of course, cold on the

Iranian plateau in the winter. Likewise, the amber desired by the Iranians was, as many people forget, not only employed for manufacturing decorative ornaments but also widely used in medicine. Thus, the Sasanians had good reason to trade with the north. I believe, however, that the export of silver to the north also had a basis in diplomacy.

One of the policies of the Sasanian emperor Kavad, and of his son and successor Chosroes I, seems to have been the development of the Caspian provinces and Gurgan to the east of the Caspian Sea. The important seaport of Abaskun was reportedly founded by Kavad; later, under Chosroes, the great wall of Gurgan (today Kızıl Yılan, "the red snake") was built to protect the province from raids by nomads. Limited space prevents discussion here of the many problems related to the nomads who threatened the northern borders of the Sasanian empire, both east and west of the Caspian Sea. Suffice it to say that all the northern borders of the empire were threatened by Turkic-speaking peoples or their allies. Chosroes I was very busy in the Transcaucasian region, including Derbent, and in Gurgan, seeking to defend Iran against her northern foes as well as to expand his territories.

This brings us to the diplomatic basis for the Sasanian trade with the north. Just as the Romans, and especially the Byzantines, had sought allies in the steppes of southern Russia against the nomadic foes threatening their borders, so did the Sasanians seek support in lands to the north against enemies who would invade their empire. Likewise, just as the cities of the Crimea and Azov Sea, once Greek, provided a base for Byzantine diplomatic and commercial activities, so the Iranian traders and settlements in southern Russia provided contacts for Sasanian diplomatic and commercial plans. I suggest that the Sasanians themselves knew little if anything about the peoples of northern Russia; it was the merchants in southern Russia who acted as middlemen between Sasanian Iran and the north, for it was surely in their commercial interest to promote exchanges.

When we turn to the smaller numbers of Byzantine silver plates and bowls found in the Kama region, the variety of subjects decorating them is less striking than their number and their date. Leonid A. Matsulevich, who studied their decoration, noted that at least twenty-five Byzantine silver plates and bowls had been found in the Kama region—almost twice as many as those discovered elsewhere in Russia. More important still, from my point of view, he determined that almost all of these objects dated from the end of the sixth and the seventh century and had probably been shipped directly to the Kama region, where they were promptly buried. These dates correspond to those of the Sasanian silver discovered in the Kama area, although the dating of "Sasanian-style" silver plates is more difficult than that of their Byzantine counterparts. A control for such dating is provided by a hoard of Byzantine coins dating from the reign of Heraclius (610–641) found in a Sasanian bowl in the village of Bartym in 1950. Other indices, such as inscriptions on the objects, also confirm the dating of most of both Byzantine and Sasanian silver objects to the end of the sixth and through the seventh century.

The picture painted by the distribution and dating of the silver plates coincides remarkably with the evidence of silver coins. We know that Heraclius minted a great amount of silver *miliaresia,* or hexagrams, for the Persian wars in the 620s. These have been found in considerable quantities in Transcaucasia, but in Russia they are limited to the Kama region, with a scattering north of the Caucasus and none in other parts of European Russia. The monetary situation in Transcaucasia was complicated, but in general one could say that the Byzantine gold *solidus* was the basis of the money economy of Lazica, on the Black Sea coast. In Georgia, both Byzantine and Sasanian coins circulated, and in Arran (Albania) and Armenia, the Sasanian *dirhams* dominated the market. Thus, it is reasonable to assume that the silver coins circulated in Transcaucasia, while in the Kama region they were hoarded.

The dating of both the plates and the coins points to two con-
clusions. First, the end of the sixth and most of the seventh century saw an expansion of both Byzantine and Sasanian contacts
with the north; and second, the people of the Kama region at
this time imported silver in great quantities. I have already mentioned the importance of silver objects in the cult of the local
people, but it can hardly be assumed that this was an innovation
in the sixth century, for writers in the nineteenth mention as still
current the custom of dedicating silver objects to deities and
spirits of the pagan tribes. We may assume, therefore, that both
the Byzantines and the Sasanian Persians "discovered" the
north in the sixth century. Alternatively, one might say that the
peoples of the Kama "discovered" the south in this period, and
with it, a source of silver objects from Byzantium and Iran.

Fortunately, the beginnings of trade in the Kama area have
been investigated by Valentin L. Yanin, who concluded that this
area and the region along the Ural Mountains were the first cor-
ners of Eastern Europe to be opened to trade with the east, since
they had already assumed this role in the sixth century. Archaeologists tell us that the first towns in Eastern Europe were
located in northeastern Russia. On the Kama River, towns were
built long before the rise of Kiev or Novgorod. The fascinating
vistas opened by the finds of silver objects and coins in northeastern Russia, added to archaeological excavations, will enable
us to reconstruct the southward movement of this area's inhabitants in the aftermath of the Hunnish invasions, when the
Goths, Alans, and others evacuated southern Russia and left a
vacuum. It is not my purpose, nor indeed my competence, to
discuss problems of the history of Russia, but the silver finds fit
well with the events of that history.

They are likewise consistent with the history of Byzantium
and Iran. At the end of the sixth century the trade between
Byzantium and India shifted from Mesopotamia (in Sasanian
territory) to the Red Sea and western Arabian routes. In 568 a
Turkish mission arrived in Constantinople to establish trade

contacts north of the Caspian Sea, to be followed by other embassies. From this, it appears that the Byzantines were seeking to open new trade routes to India and China by avoiding any passage through Sasanian territory, where they would be subject to attack by their enemies. The Sasanians' response was to attempt to cut off these new trade routes by expanding their realm, acquiring new bases from which they could attack Byzantine merchants. The Sasanians occupied Yemen after 570, and Chosroes I made attempts to expand into Lazica in Transcaucasia and into Hephtalite territory in the northeast. The competition in trade between the two empires opened new markets and also increased older contacts with regions such as the Kama area of Russia.

The role of the peoples of northeastern Russia in the diplomatic and commercial activities of the two great powers was small, probably decidedly secondary, and managed through the intervention of middlemen to the south. One could not say that these peoples played any decisive role in the drama of conflict between Byzantium and Sasanian Iran. Nonetheless, they did play a small part in this great struggle and undoubtedly provided a background for the later Viking expansion down the Volga River.

In sum, the mystery of the Kama silver appears to be solvable in light of these two pieces of information: the internal history and customs of the native people of the Kama, and the commercial and diplomatic rivalry between the Byzantines and the Sasanians in the sixth century. The people of the Kama region eagerly sought silver because of their religious practices, and the Byzantines and Sasanians eagerly supplied it because of their desire to surpass each other in trade and diplomatic contacts.

Bibliography

Translations and texts of Ibn Fadlan (complete or partial)

Blake, Robert P., and Richard N. Frye. 1949. "Notes on the Risala of Ibn Fadlan." *Byzantina-Metabyzantina* 1 (part 2): 7–37. (Reproduced in Frye, 1979. *Islamic Iran and Central Asia*. London: Variorum Reprints.)

Canard, Marius. 1958. "La relation du voyage d'Ibn Fadlan chez les Bulgares." *Annales de l'Institut d'Etudes Orientales* 5:41–146.

Czeglédy, Károly. 1951. "Zur Meschheder Handschrift von Ibn Fadlan's Reisebericht." *Acta Orientalia* 5:218–60.

Dahan, Sami. 1959. *Risalah fi wasf al-rihalah 'ila bilad al-turk wa al-rus wa al-saqaliba*. Damascus.

Fraehn, Christian M. 1823. *Ibn Fozlans und andere Araber Berichte über die alten Russen älterer Zeit*. St. Petersburg.

Kovalevskii, A. P. 1956. *Kniga Akhmeda Ibn-Fadlana o ego Puteshestvii na Volgu 921–922 gg*. Kharkov.

Kovalevskii, A. P. 1939. *Puteshestvie Ibn Fadlana na Volgu*. Moscow.

Shamsi, Sultan. 1992. *Puteshestvie Ibn Fadlana na reku Itil*. Kazan.

Togan, Zeki-Velidi A. 1939. *Ibn Fadlan's Reisebericht*. Vol. 24, part 3 of *Abhandlungen für die Kunde des Morgenlands*. Leipzig.

Related publications

Bolshakov, Oleg G., and Aleksandr L. Mongait. 1971. *Puteshestvie Abu Khamida al-Garnati v vostochnuyu i tsentralnuyu Evropu*. Moscow.

Brook, Kevin A. 1999. *The Jews of Khazaria*. Northvale, New Jersey: J. Aronson.

Coon, Carleton S. 1948. *A Reader in General Anthropology*. New York: Holt.

Dubler, César E. 1953. *Abu Hamid el Granadino y su relación de viaje por tierras Euroasiáticas.* Madrid: Maestre.

Dunlop, Douglas M. 1954. *History of the Jewish Khazars.* Princeton, New Jersey: Princeton University Press.

Frye, Richard N. 1972. "Byzantine and Sasanian Trade with N.E. Russia." *Dumbarton Oaks Papers* 26:265–69.

Frye, Richard N., ed. 1974. "Methodology in Iranian History." *Neue Methodologie in der Iranistik.* Wiesbaden: Harrasowitz.

Gignoux, Phil. 1971. "L'inscription de Kirdir a Naqsh-i Rostam." *Studia Iranica* 1:177–206.

Golb, Norman, and Omeljan Pritsak. 1982. *Khazarian Hebrew Documents of the Tenth Century.* Ithaca, N.Y.: Cornell University Press.

Jacob, Georg. 1887. *Der nordisch-baltische Handel der Araber im Mittelalter.* Leipzig: G. Böhme.

Laufer, Berthold. 1919. *Sino-Iranica: Chinese Contributions to the History of Civilization in Ancient Iran.* Chicago: Field Museum of Natural History.

Markwart, Josef M. 1924. "Ein arabischer Bericht über die arktischen (Uralischen) Länder aus dem 10. Jahrhundert." *Ungarische Jahrbücher* 4:261–334.

Montgomery, James E. 2000. "Ibn Fadlan and the Rusiyyah." *Journal of Arabic and Islamic Studies* 3 (2000). http://www.uib.no/jais/content3.htm.

Pritsak, Omeljan. 1998. *The Origins of the Old Rus´ Weights and Monetary Systems.* Cambridge, Mass.: Harvard University Press.

Pritsak, Omeljan. 1980. *The Origin of Rus´.* Cambridge, Mass.: Harvard University Press.

Ritter, Hellmut. 1942. "Zum Text von Ibn Fadlan's Reisebericht." *Zeitschrift der Deutschen Morgenländischen Gesellschaft* 96:98–126.

Schafer, Edward. 1963. *The Golden Peaches of Samarkand.* Berkeley, Calif.: University of California Press.

Vaissière, Etienne de la. 2002. *Histoire des marchands sogdiens.* Paris: Boccard.

Wüstenfeld, Ferdinand, ed. 1866–73. *Jacut's Geographisches Wörterbuch [Geographical Dictionary of Yaqut].* Leipzig: F. A. Brockhaus.

Illustration Sources

p. i: Ships of the Rus, miniature in the Radzivilovskoi ms., 16th c.; p. 1: Princeton University Library (original in the Hermitage Museum, St. Petersburg); p. 2: map by Tsering Wangyal Shawa, Geographic Information Systems Librarian, Princeton University; pp. 6, 17, 91, 151: maps and diagrams from Maurice Lombard, *The Golden Age of Islam* (Princeton: Markus Wiener, 2004); p. 11: B.I. Marshak, *Sogdiiskoe Serebro* (Moscow, 1971), plate T-31; p. 12: map by Martin Gamache/Alpine Mapping Guild; p. 18: Leo Bagrow, *Geschichte der Kartographie* (Berlin: Safari Verlag, 1944, 1951); p. 23: *Zur Geschichte der Kostüme* (Munich: Braun & Schneider, 1861–1880); pp. 14, 27, 31, 38, 55, 86, 89: photos by Richard Frye; p. 48: L.I. Albaum, *Zhivopis' Afrasiyaba* (Tashkent, 1975), 49; pp. 51, 75, 134: S.A. Pletneva, *Die Chasaren: Mittelalterliches Reich an Don und Wolga* (Leipzig: VPB, 1978); pp. 64, 108, 104, 128: collection of the publisher; p. 78: *Anglo-Saxon Chronicle*, trans. D. Whitelock, English Historical Documents, vol. 1, 1955; p. 115: *Maqamat of al-Hariri*, collection of the author; p. 124: Bertold Spuler, *The Mongol Period* (Princeton: Markus Wiener, 1994), p. XIX; p. 143: *Xinjiangdin kezieelinqan medini yadikarliklar* (Xinjiang ancient cultural relics) (Beijing, 1975).

About the Author

Richard N. Frye is professor emeritus of Near Eastern Languages and Civilization at Harvard University, where he was the
Aga Khan Professor of Iranian. He is the author of numerous
books, including *Bukhara: The Medieval Achievement; The History
of Ancient Iran; The Golden Age of Persia: The Arabs in the East;
Greater Iran: A 20th-century Odyssey* (his memoirs); *The Heritage
of Central Asia: From Antiquity to the Turkish Expansion;* and *The
Near East and the Great Powers.*

Lightning Source UK Ltd.
Milton Keynes UK
UKHW011347231020
372105UK00001B/3